Badger Key Stage 4
Maths Starters

Year 11

Brian Fillis

You may copy this book freely for use in your school.
The pages in this book are copyright, but copies may be made without fees or prior permission provided that these copies are used only by the institution which purchased the book. For copying in any other circumstances, prior written consent must be obtained from the publisher.

Badger Publishing

Introduction

The starters featured in this book are designed to support teachers in building on the work that students have done at Key Stage 3. The aim is to consolidate concepts met previously and move rapidly to developing the new skills that will move students on to the GCSE. They are written to cover the four aspects of mathematics at Foundation and Higher level and are graded to support pitch and differentiation in the classroom.

Crucially, they may be used to develop independent learning skills in the students. They frequently require students to grade new mathematical concepts for themselves, and to decide what constitutes a 'challenging' exam skill – what makes it challenging in the first place. They are then encouraged to assess their own progress and decide what they need to do to move to the next level.

Finally, I hope they support the development of thinking and problem-solving skills in the students. The starters in the fourth section, Handling data, have been designed for use in launching the GCSE data-handling coursework and should be used to structure the teaching of the project.

Brian Fillis

Badger KS4 Maths Starters
Year 11 ISBN 1 84424 642 6

Text © Brian Fillis 2006
Complete work © Badger Publishing Limited 2006

The right of Brian Fillis to be identified as author of this Work has been asserted by him in accordance with the Copyright, Designs and Patents Act 1988.

Badger Publishing Limited
15 Wedgwood Gate,
Pin Green Industrial Estate,
Stevenage,
Hertfordshire SG1 4SU
Telephone: 01438 356907
Fax: 01438 747015
www.badger-publishing.co.uk
enquiries@badger-publishing.co.uk

Publisher: David Jamieson
Editor: Paul Martin
Designer: Adam Wilmott
Illustrator: Adam Wilmott

Printed in the UK

Contents

Number
1. Multiply and divide simple fractions
2. Add and subtract fractions
3. Equivalence between fractions and percentages
4. One quantity as a percentage of another
5. Percentage problems
6. Percentages: increases and decreases
7. Simplify a ratio
8. Divide a quantity in a given ratio
9. Use a calculator
10. Estimate answers
11. Upper and lower bounds
12. Percentage changes: decimal multipliers
13. Find the original amount after a percentage change
14. The rules of indices
15. Fractional and negative indices
16. Standard index notation
17. Reciprocals
18. Irrational numbers
19. Exponential growth and decay

Algebra
20. Substitute into expressions and formulae
21. Solve equations
22. Factorise
23. Plot graphs
24. Real-life, distance/time and conversion graphs
25. Find the gradient and y-intercept
26. Draw a straight-line graph by using m and c
27. Expand and simplify linear expressions
28. Factorise a quadratic
29. Plot quadratic and cubic curves
30. Solve quadratics
31. The difference of two squares
32. Simplify algebraic fractions
33. Solve simultaneous equations
34. Linear inequalities
35. The curves $y = \sin x$, $y = \cos x$ and $y = \tan x$
36. Graphs such as $y = a + b \sin x$
37. The graphs of $y = f(x) + a$, $y = f(ax)$, $y = f(x + a)$, and $y = af(x)$
38. Express a circle in algebraic form
39. Solve a pair of simultaneous equations (one non-linear)
40. Calculate where a straight-line graph meets a circle

Shape, space and measures

41. Translate simple 2D shapes
42. Corresponding and alternate angles
43. Properties of a parallelogram
44. Triangle proofs
45. Describe solid shapes
46. Draw nets of simple solids
47. The circumference of a circle
48. The area of a circle
49. Convert between units of area or volume
50. Similar shapes
51. Pythagoras' theorem
52. Trigonometry 1
53. Trigonometry 2
54. Trigonometry and Pythagoras problems
55. Trig in three dimensions
56. Loci constructions 1
57. Loci constructions 2
58. Circle theorems
59. Length, area or volume formulae
60. Length, area or volume scale factors

Handling data

61. Suggest a complex hypothesis
62. Plan an enquiry
63. Take a sample
64. Two-way tables
65. Compare correlations
66. Estimates for the mean and median
67. Compare two distributions
68. Use cumulative frequency curves
69. Compare two box-plot diagrams
70. Time series
71. Moving averages
72. Draw histograms
73. Interpret histograms
74. Relative frequencies
75. Tree diagrams
76. The '**AND**' rule
77. The '**OR**' rule
78. Conditional probability

Year 11 Maths Starter 1
Multiply and divide simple fractions

Number

Objective:
Multiply and divide simple fractions where the answers may involve mixed numbers.

Grade: F/E

What you will need:
OHT 1

Time:
5-10 minutes

Key words:
multiply, multiplied by, divide, divided by, fraction, half, quarter, sixth

Activity:
Ask the students:

Q: What's a half of 6? If I multiply $\frac{1}{2}$ by 6, will I get the same answer? If I add six halves together? So 'a half of six' is the same as '$\frac{1}{2}$ multiplied by 6'. What's $\frac{1}{2}$ multiplied by $\frac{1}{4}$?

Give students 1-2 minutes to discuss the problem in pairs.

Q: What thoughts did you have? Does it help to think of the problem as a half of a quarter? If we cut a quarter in half, what fraction would we have then?

Show OHT 1.

Q: How could we use the first diagram to help? If we shade in the half of a quarter? How many of these could we get into one whole? (Eight) What do you notice about the solution to $\frac{1}{2} \times \frac{1}{4}$ What do you think $\frac{1}{2} \times \frac{1}{5}$ will be? Why?

Refer to the second diagram.

Q: How could we use this diagram to solve the calculation $\frac{1}{2} \div \frac{1}{6}$?

Links to plenary:
How did you complete $\frac{1}{2} \div \frac{1}{6}$? What's the solution to the calculation $\frac{1}{2} \times \frac{6}{1}$? What do you notice? What is $\frac{6}{2}$? As an integer? What do I mean by 'integer'? How does this help us to establish a method for dividing fractions?

Badger Key Stage 4 Maths Starters

© Badger Publishing Ltd

Year 11: Copymaster for Starter 1 (OHT)

Multiply and divide simple fractions

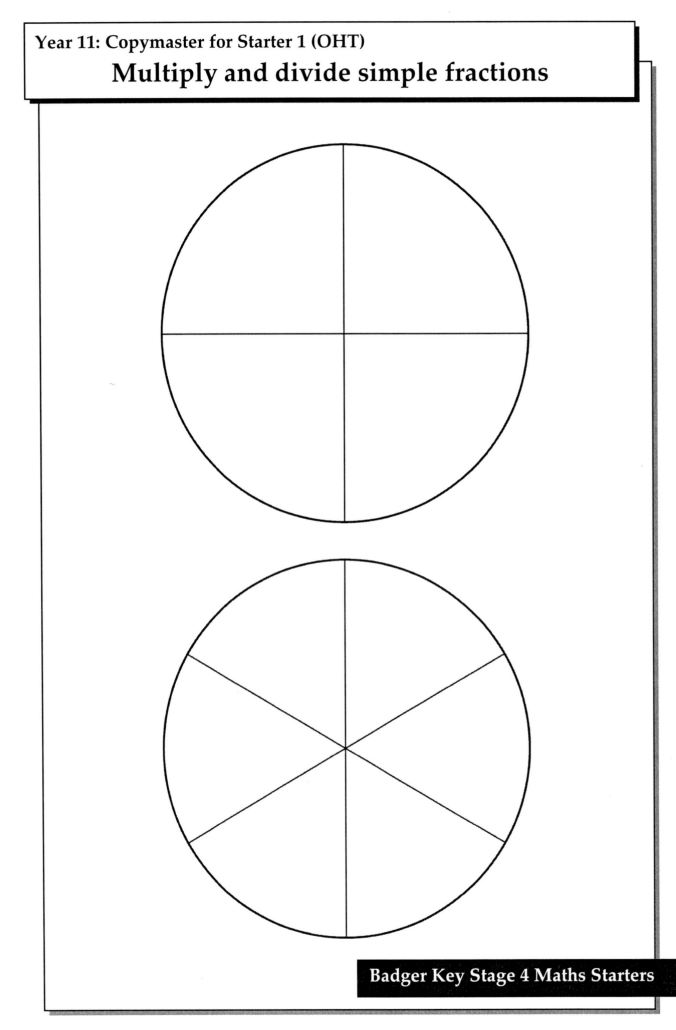

Badger Key Stage 4 Maths Starters

© Badger Publishing Ltd

Year 11 Maths Starter 2 — Number

Add and subtract fractions

Objective:

Add and subtract fractions including simple cases involving mixed numbers.

Grade: D

What you will need:
OHT 2

Time:
5-10 minutes

Key words:

fraction, add, subtract, numerator, denominator, multiple, lowest common multiple

Activity:

Show OHT 2. Explain that the aim is to use the diagram to do the calculation $\frac{1}{4}+\frac{1}{3}+\frac{1}{6}$.

Q: Why have I put up a rectangle divided into twelfths? How will that help us with the calculation? Why didn't I put up a rectangle divided into fifteenths? Why is twelve useful for this particular calculation? How can we use the diagram? If we want to shade a quarter of the rectangle, how many twelfths will that be? What's the solution to the calculation?

Give students 1-2 minutes to solve the problem in pairs.

Links to plenary:

Q: What did you get? Could we have performed the calculation without the rectangle diagram? If we wanted to do the calculation $\frac{2}{5}+\frac{1}{10}$, what rectangle diagram would we need? Into how many equal parts would it be divided? Why? How could we adapt this method to find one for subtracting fractions?

Badger Key Stage 4 Maths Starters

Year 11: Copymaster for Starter 2 (OHT)
Add and subtract fractions

Badger Key Stage 4 Maths Starters

Year 11 Maths Starter 3

Number

Equivalence between fractions and percentages

Objective:

Recognise equivalence between simple fractions and percentages.

Grade: F/E

What you will need:
No additional resources.

Time:
5-10 minutes

Key words:

equivalent, equivalence, fraction, decimal, percentage

Activity:

Ask the students:

Q: Can someone give me a fraction and a percentage that are equivalent? What do I mean by 'equivalent'? What pair are very easy to think of? Why is it easy to identify $\frac{1}{2}$ and 50% as an equivalent pair? What other easy pairs can you think of? I want you now to work in pairs and write down as many equivalent pairs of fractions and percentages as you can think of.

Give students 3-4 minutes to attempt the activity.

Q: What did you come up with? Which were easy to identify as pairs? How was $\frac{1}{4}$ and 25% easy? Is it easy to divide 100 by 4? What other numbers will divide easily into 100? How does that help? Which pairs were harder to find? What makes them harder? Did anyone find the percentage equivalent for $\frac{1}{3}$? How? True or false: 'Some fractions don't have percentage equivalents'?

Links to plenary:

Q: How do we find the percentage equivalent for $\frac{1}{6}$? What's $\frac{1}{2}$ as a decimal? How do we change 0.5 into 50? How can we adapt that method to find the percentage equivalent for $\frac{1}{6}$?

Badger Key Stage 4 Maths Starters

© Badger Publishing Ltd

Year 11 Maths Starter 4 — Number

One quantity as a percentage of another

Objective:

Give one quantity as a percentage of another.

Grade: F/E

What you will need:
OHT 4

Time:
5-10 minutes

Key words:
equivalent, equivalence, fraction, decimal, percentage, convert

Activity:

Ask the students:

Q: Imagine a box of 20 light bulbs. Upon testing, we find out that 5 of them are broken. What percentage of the bulbs are broken? How did you work it out? What made the problem relatively easy? Why did the numbers 5 and 20 make it easy? Would it have been harder if I'd said 6 out of 20 were broken? Why? How could we give $\frac{6}{20}$ as a percentage? Can we easily convert $\frac{6}{20}$ into a fraction out of 100? Isn't that what a percentage *is* ~ a fraction out of 100?

How do we convert $\frac{6}{20}$ into a fraction out of 100? Is 30% less than $\frac{1}{3}$ or more than $\frac{1}{3}$? So: the numbers 6 and 20 were relatively easy. What if there were 21 bulbs in the box and 6 were broken?

Give students 3-4 minutes to solve the problem in pairs. Then set them problems from the target board on OHT 4. They are to choose a quantity from board 1 and give it as a percentage of another quantity chosen from board 2. Encourage more able students to choose challenging pairs of quantities.

Links to plenary:

Q: How can we convert $\frac{6}{21}$ into a decimal? Is it appropriate to use a calculator? How do we do the conversion? What do we do next? Will the percentage be larger than 30%? Why? Which pairs did you choose from the target boards? Which were easy and which challenging? How did you convert the more challenging pairs?

Badger Key Stage 4 Maths Starters

© Badger Publishing Ltd

Year 11: Copymaster for Starter 4 (OHT)

One quantity as a percentage of another

Two target boards

5	28
9	6
4	3

36	40
63	42
35	18

Badger Key Stage 4 Maths Starters

Year 11 Maths Starter 5 — Number

Percentage problems

Objective:

Use percentages to solve problems involving VAT, taxation, bills, profit and loss.

Grade: E/D

What you will need:
OHT 5

Time:
5-10 minutes

Key words:
percentage, quantity, cost price, sale price, VAT, profit, loss

Activity:

Show OHT 5.

Q: Look at this problem. What grade do you think it's pitched at? (Grade E/D) If this is a question on the calculator paper, what makes it worth a D grade? What aspects of maths does it involve? Are there any words in the problem that don't immediately make sense? What are 'overheads'? What does '50% mark up on the cost price' mean? What do we need to work out first? If the company sells one DVD a month, will it make a profit? Why not? If there were no overheads? What profit would it make?

Give students 1 minute to work this out.

Q: What profit does the company make on one DVD? (£2) How did you work it out? Have we solved the problem? What else do we have to do? How can we use the calculator?

Give students another minute to find the solution to the question.

Links to plenary:

Q: How did you do it? What calculation did you use? What operation? Why is this a division problem? How many £2s do we need to make to cover the overheads? (600) Does that mean we make a profit? So what's the solution? Could we have solved this problem without a calculator?

Badger Key Stage 4 Maths Starters

© Badger Publishing Ltd

Percentage problems

A company sells DVDs.

In one month, it has to pay £1200 in overheads.

Each DVD costs £4 to make.

They sell DVDs with a 50% mark up on the cost price.

What is the smallest number of DVDs that they have to sell in a month to make a profit?

Year 11 Maths Starter 6 — Number
Percentages: increases and decreases

Objective:
Understand and use equivalence between fractions, decimals and percentages; cancel fractions.

Grade: D/C

What you will need:
OHT 6

Time:
5-10 minutes

Key words:
percentage, fraction, simplify, lowest terms, quantity, profit, loss, increase, decrease

Activity:

Show OHT 6. Ask the students:

Q: Are these two shops being equally generous in the way that they've cut their prices? Why might shop A be able to say that their reduction is identical to shop B? How could we explain that, in fact, shop B is cutting its price in a much bigger way?

Give students 1 minute to discuss this in pairs.

Q: Are they the same reduction? What makes these reductions different? How could we use maths to show that the second reduction is a much larger decrease? Do shops show reductions as fractions of the original price? How? What fraction of the price has been slashed at shop B? Roughly what is £10 as a fraction of £45? Is it less than or more than a quarter?

How can we give it as an exact fraction? Is it $\frac{10}{45}$? Can we simplify that fraction? What is it in its lowest terms? Work out what 10 is as a fraction of 300.

Links to plenary:

Q: So the reductions can be written as $\frac{1}{30}$ and $\frac{2}{9}$. Why is that not a good way of comparing the two reductions? Would a shop put an ad in the window reading 'Two ninths off everything'? What would they do? How can we convert these fractions into percentage decreases?

Badger Key Stage 4 Maths Starters

© Badger Publishing Ltd

Percentages: increases and decreases

Shop A

A DVD recorder

Was: £300
Now: £290

Shop B

A DVD player

Was: £45
Now: £35

Year 11 Maths Starter 7　　　　　　　　　　　　　　　　　　　　**Number**

Simplify a ratio

Objective:
Simplify a ratio by dividing both its numbers by a common factor; recognise when a ratio is in its lowest terms.

Grade: D

What you will need:
OHT 7

Time:
5-10 minutes

Key words:
ratio, equivalent, factor, common factor, highest common factor, lowest terms

Activity:

Show OHT 7. Ask the students:

Q: What does this target board show? What is featured in each of the cells? Is it enough to say that they are 'ratios'? What is being shown by these ratios? What are 'ratios' made of? Could we describe them as pairs of numbers? Are the pairs being related to each other in some way? Imagine these are teacher : student ratios. Which one might show a student working at home with a private tutor? (1:1) Are any of these ratios equivalent? What do I mean by 'equivalent'? How can we identify equivalent ratios? See if you can find two pairs of equivalent ratios.

Give students 2-3 minutes to attempt this.

Q: Which did you find? Which were easy to spot? What made them easy to spot? How did you confirm that they were equivalent? Did you simplify them? What do I mean by 'simplify'? How did you do that? Did anyone simplify the ratio 21 : 14? What did you do? Why divide by 7? Is 7 a factor of both numbers? How does that help? Look at the exam question at the bottom of the OHT. Has the student found the correct solution?

Links to plenary:

Q: What's wrong with the solution? Has the student found a common factor of 16 and 40? What common factor? Has the student given the ratio in its lowest terms? What do we have to do? What common factor should the student have chosen? How can we make sure we've given the ration in its lowest terms?

Badger Key Stage 4 Maths Starters

© Badger Publishing Ltd

Year 11: Copymaster for Starter 7 (OHT)
Simplify a ratio

21 : 35	3 : 2	6 : 8
21 : 14	1 : 1	3 : 7
6 : 10	12 : 16	3 : 4
9 : 6	9 : 21	16 : 18

Give the ratio 16 : 40 in its lowest terms:

$16 \div 4 = 8$ and $40 \div 4 = 10$ so it's

8 : 10 in its lowest terms.

Answer .... 8 : 10   (2 marks)

Badger Key Stage 4 Maths Starters

Year 11 Maths Starter 8 — Number

Divide a quantity in a given ratio

Objective:

Divide a quantity in a given ratio.

Grade: D

What you will need:
OHT 8

Time:
5-10 minutes

Key words:

ratio, quantity, lowest terms, factor

Activity:

Explain to the students that you are going to set a problem that involves dividing a quantity into a ratio.

Q: What would be a really simple quantity to divide? Why might 40 or 60 or 100 be easy quantities to divide? What is the simplest ratio that we could possibly divide a quantity in?

Why is 1 : 1 the simplest? What's £60 divided in the ratio 1 : 1? How many sums of money do we end up with? By what number did you divide 60? OK. How could we adapt that method to divide £60 in the ratio 1 : 2?

Give the students 1-2 minutes to discuss this.

Q: How could we do it? How many sums of money will we end up with? Why is it still two sums of money? Is the £60 being shared equally this time? Will the second sum be twice the size of the first? What do we divide £60 by now? Why three?
So £60 ÷ 3 = £20. What next?

Have we solved the problem?

Show OHT 8. Give students 4-5 minutes to devise ratio problems, choosing a quantity from one target board and a ratio from the second.

Links to plenary:

Q: Which problems did you devise? What made the simple problems easy? What made some of them more challenging? Why might dividing £18 in the ratio 4 : 5 be easier than dividing it in the ratio 1 : 3? Did the procedure change? Was the method always the same? How do we remember this method?

Badger Key Stage 4 Maths Starters

© Badger Publishing Ltd

Year 11: Copymaster for Starter 8 (OHT)

Divide a quantity in a given ratio

100	164	66
42	49	105
45	28	22

2 : 1	5 : 2	1 : 5
2 : 3	3 : 1	4 : 3
4 : 5	1 : 4	4 : 7

Badger Key Stage 4 Maths Starters

© Badger Publishing Ltd

Year 11 Maths Starter 9

Number

Use a calculator

Objective:

Use a calculator effectively and interpret the calculator display.

Grade: E/D

What you will need:
OHT 9, class set of calculators.

Time:
5-10 minutes

Key words:
calculate, calculator, multiply, divide, subtract, add

Activity:

Ask the students:

Q: Why do you think that you are permitted a calculator for one of the exam papers but not the other? What skills do you think are being assessed on the non-calculator paper? What about the calculator paper? If you are allowed a calculator, does that make it an easier paper? What skills might make the calculator paper more challenging?

Show OHT 9. Ask the students to identify problems that would appear on the calculator paper, and those that would appear on the non-calculator paper. Give them 3-4 minutes to discuss in pairs.

Q: Which problems can we solve without a calculator? How? Would a multiplication like 45 x 67 be a calculator question? Why not? What about the calculation in the bottom left cell? How would we use the calculator to solve this? What skill is being assessed? Why is the word problem likely to be a calculator problem? Are the numbers 'difficult' ones? Will it involve multiplication and division? What operations should we use to solve the problem? Is that the difficult part? Deciding what operations to use? How can we make that easier?

Give students 2-3 minutes to plan a solution.

Links to plenary:

Q: How did you do it? What was the first calculation you needed to do? Why a subtraction? What does the answer represent in this context? What did you do then? Why divide? Talk me through the steps you went through to solve the second part of the question.

Badger Key Stage 4 Maths Starters

© Badger Publishing Ltd

Use a calculator

45 × 67	714 ÷ 17
Increase £450 by 20%	A trader buys 400 DVDs for £300. She sells all the DVDs over the internet. She charges £2 each for a single disc or packs of 5 discs for £9. She sells 165 single discs ~ the remaining discs are sold in packs of 5. How many packs of 5 does she sell? What profit does she make?
Decrease 1617g by 23%	Find an approximate value for the solution to the equation $x^3 = 43$.
$\dfrac{4.04 \times 3.2}{16.7 - 0.78}$	7000 − 199

Year 11 Maths Starter 10 — Number

Estimate answers

Objective:
Use one significant figure to estimate answers without a calculator.

Grade: C

What you will need:
OHT 10

Time: 5-10 minutes

Key words:
approximate, estimate, round, decimal place, significant figure

Activity:
Ask the students:

Q: What's an approximate answer to the calculation $1.0001 - 0.999$? Can you give me a one digit estimate of the solution? How did you find it? What kind of rounding did you do? Why did you round both numbers to one significant figure? What do I mean by 'one significant figure'?

OK. Let's imagine we are the examiner. We want to devise a problem that will assess the students abilities to round to one significant figure and make an estimate of a calculation. The approximation that the students will need to do will be 4×0.5, giving the estimate: 2. What could the original 'difficult' calculation be?

Give students 1-2 minutes to devise a problem for which $4 \times 0.5 = 2$ gives the approximation.

Q: How did you do it? Could a different estimate for your calculation be made? How?

Show OHT 10. Give students 2 minutes to attempt to find an estimate for the solution.

Links to plenary:

Q: How did you solve this problem? What estimates did you come up with? Why are some estimates different? Why might it be sensible to break the rules relating to approximation with this question? Why might it be useful to round the 65 down to 60 rather than up to 70?

Badger Key Stage 4 Maths Starters

Year 11: Copymaster for Starter 10 (OHT)

Estimate answers

Find an estimate to the calculation

$$65 \div (10.7 - 8.26)$$

Answer . . . . *(3 marks)*

Year 11 Maths Starter 11 — Number

Upper and lower bounds

Objective:

Begin to recognise simple examples of upper and lower bounds.

Grade: C

What you will need:
OHT 11, class set of calculators.

Time:
5-10 minutes

Key words:
approximate, estimate, round, decimal place, significant figure, upper and lower bound

Activity:

Ask the students:

Q: Give me a number with two decimal places that would round to 12 to the nearest unit. Who gave me a number lower than 12? Can someone give me a number that's smaller than that one? How low can we go? What's the smallest number with two decimal places that will round up to 12? (11.51) Why can we not include 11.5 in this context? To what would 11.49 round? What's the largest number that will round down to 12? What grade do you think identifying the upper and lower bounds of a rounded number is? What do I mean by 'upper and lower bounds'?

Show OHT 11. Prompt students to attempt the two problems. Give them 4-5 minutes.

Links to plenary:

Q: Why might it be possible to find two different solutions ~ a largest and a smallest? What solutions did you find for the first problem? How did you do it? Why was the second problem more challenging? What's the solution to the division 60 ÷ 2? How about 60 ÷ 3? How is it that, by increasing the divisor, we get a smaller answer? How might that help us to get the smallest answer to problem 2?

Badger Key Stage 4 Maths Starters

© Badger Publishing Ltd

Year 11: Copymaster for Starter 11 (OHT)

Upper and lower bounds

The numbers in each of these calculations were numbers with one decimal place before they were rounded to the nearest unit.

For each of the calculations, find the largest possible solution and the smallest possible.

1   45 × 16

2   60 ÷ 8

Year 11 Maths Starter 12
Number
Percentage changes: decimal multipliers

Objective:
Write down a decimal multiplier which is equivalent to an increase or decrease by a given percentage; e.g. that an increase of 15% is equivalent to multiplying by 1.15.

Grade: D/C/B

What you will need:
Class set of calculators.

Time:
5-10 minutes

Key words:
percentage, equivalent, multiplier, increase

Activity:
Ask the students:

Q: Increase £300 by 50%. OK. Multiply £300 by 1.5. What do you notice? Why do these both give the same solution?

Give students 1-2 minutes to discuss this in pairs.

Q: Why do they give the same solution? What effect does the 1 in the units column have in the calculation £300 x 1.5? Does this ensure that we 'keep' the original £300 in our solution? What about the .5 part of the multiplier? What do I mean by 'multiplier'? What single multiplier is equivalent to an increase by 20%? How could we test this? Can we solve any increase problem by using a single multiplier? When might it be easier than using a mental method like the one we know? OK. I've thought of a number. What letter symbol shall we give for this unknown number? OK. I've increased the number by 20%. It's now 54. What *was* the original number?

Give students 1-2 minutes to discuss this in pairs.

Links to plenary:

Q: What did you come up with? Did you use a calculator? Did anyone write an equation? How did the equation read? What makes this equation look complex when compared to the ones we are familiar with? How do we solve it? What grade do you think this kind of question corresponds to? (B) Does that surprise you?

Badger Key Stage 4 Maths Starters

© Badger Publishing Ltd

Year 11 Maths Starter 13 — Number

Find the original amount after a percentage change

Objective:
Find the original amount, e.g. price before a sale, price before VAT.

Grade: B

What you will need:
Class set of calculators.

Time:
5-10 minutes

Key words:
percentage increase, decrease, sale price, cost price, multiplier

Activity:
Ask the students:

Q: What single multiplier is equivalent to a percentage increase by 50%? I want to increase 300kg by 50%. What single multiplication can I do? Why will it be x 1.5? OK. I've thought of an amount. I've increased it by 50%. It's now 225. What was it before I increased it?

Give students 2-3 minutes to discuss this in pairs.

Q: Did anyone come up with a solution? (150) How did you find that value? Who decided to work out 50% of 225 and subtract it? Will that give us the solution? How could we test this solution? Was it the 225 I found 50% of or the original amount? How can we work backwards to find out the unknown that I began with? Can algebra help us with this? What if we label the original amount 'x'? Can we write an equation? How does the single multiplier help us?

How do we solve the equation? OK. Do we now have this grade B skill or should we practice it? I want you, in pairs, to devise a problem for each other and then swap problems. Choose an original amount, choose a percentage increase, then find the new amount.

Give students 3-4 minutes to devise and attempt each other's problems.

Links to plenary:
Q: What if a price is decreased in a sale? What single multiplier is equivalent to a decrease by 10%? If we lose 10% of something, what percentage do we keep? What single multiplier will give us 90% of something? What single multiplier will decrease something by 15%? I think of a price. I decrease it by 15%. It's now £119. What was the price before the sale? (£140)

Badger Key Stage 4 Maths Starters

Year 11 Maths Starter 14	Number

The rules of indices

Objective:
Know the rules of indices (adding, subtracting and multiplying indices) and simplify expressions.

Grade: C/B

What you will need:
OHT 14

Time:
5-10 minutes

Key words:
power, index, indices, base number

Activity:
Ask the students:

Q: What's x multiplied by x? OK. What happens if I multiply x^2 by x? What's 3^2 multiplied by 3? If I multiply 3 to the power of 2 by 3 to the power of 1 it gives 3 to the power of 3 ~ true or false?

Show OHT 14. Refer to the first example. Ask the students to discuss the example in pairs - you are then going to ask students to explain how the example shows the index law relating to multiplication of a base number raised to indices. Give them 2-3 minutes to discuss this.

Q: Can you explain the example? What have they done first? How could we write another example to show this index law? What do I mean by 'index law'? Look at the statement 'a to the power of m x a to the power of n = ' how could we complete the statement? How does it show that the law applies to any numbers raised to any powers? True or false: $3^2 \times 7^3 = 21$ to the power of 5.

OK. What's $x^3 \div x$? Why must it be x^2? How could we complete the second example to show the second index law, relating to division?

Give students 1-2 minutes to discuss this in pairs.

Links to plenary:

Q: How did you complete the example? Can you say the rule that applies when we divide numbers raised to indices? Will this apply to any pairs of numbers? How could we use algebra to state the law in the form: a to the power of $m \div$ ...?

Badger Key Stage 4 Maths Starters

Year 11: Copymaster for Starter 14 (OHT)

The rules of indices

1 y^2 × y^3 is the same as

  $y \times y$ × $y \times y \times y$ which gives

  $y \times y \times y \times y \times y$ which is y^5

In general, a^m × a^m =

2 y^3 ÷ y^2 is the same as...

Badger Key Stage 4 Maths Starters

Year 11 Maths Starter 15 — Number

Fractional and negative indices

Objective:
Evaluate fractional and negative indices.

Grade: B/A

What you will need:
No additional resources.

Time: 5-10 minutes

Key words:
power, index, indices, base number, value

Activity:

Ask the students:

Q: What's the value of 9 to the power of $\frac{1}{2}$? We are going to try and work this out. What do we get if we multiply 9 to the power of $\frac{1}{2}$ by 9 to the power of $\frac{1}{2}$?

Give students 1-2 minutes to discuss this in pairs.

Q: What must the solution to this be? How did you find it? How did you apply the index law? What's the value of 9 to the power of 1? OK. So 9 to the power of $\frac{1}{2}$ x 9 to the power of $\frac{1}{2}$ gives us 9. So this number whose value we don't know, *when multiplied by itself*, gives us 9. What number multiplied by itself gives us 9? So what's the value of 9 to the power of $\frac{1}{2}$? OK. What's the value of 16 to the power of $\frac{1}{2}$? 25 to the power of $\frac{1}{2}$? *x* to the power of $\frac{1}{2}$?

Q: What's the value of 2 to the power of −1? How could we use the index laws to investigate?

Give students 1-2 minutes to discuss this in pairs.

Links to plenary:

Q: What can we do? What statement can we set up that includes −1? Is 2 to the power of −1 multiplied by 2 to the power of −1 going to help us? What would we get if we multiplied 2 to the power of −1 by 2 to the power of +1? What's the value of 2 to the power of +1? What's the value of 2 to the power of 0? OK. So this number, which we don't know yet, when multiplied by 2, gives us 1. What number multiplied by 2 gives us 1? What's the value of 2 to the power of −1?

Badger Key Stage 4 Maths Starters

© Badger Publishing Ltd

Year 11 Maths Starter 16   Number

Standard index notation

Objective:
Represent a number in standard form as a decimal fraction between 1 and 10 multiplied by a positive or negative power of ten; convert between standard form and 'normal' numbers; solve problems involving standard form, using the correct calculator method where possible.

Grade: B/A

What you will need:
OHT 16, class set of calculators.

Time:
5-10 minutes

Key words:
power, index, indices, standard index form

Activity:

Show OHT 16. Refer to the first statement. Give students 1-2 minutes to discuss the statement in pairs.

Q: Is the statement true or false? How did you test it? Have we changed the size of the number 342 000? Have we re-written in it in a different form? Why might this form be known as standard index form? How would we write the second number in standard index form?

Give students 1-2 minutes to attempt this in pairs.

Q: How did you do it? Why was it 10 to the power of 4 this time? Did anyone write anything different? Is your version the same size as the number 54 670? Can we have different ways of writing a number in standard index form, or should we all agree on one specific way of doing it? Is that why it's called 'standard'?

Refer to the third statement.

Links to plenary:

Q: How did you test it? Have we changed the size of the number 0.0029? How have we used what we know about negative indices to help re-write this? How could we complete the fourth problem? What grade do you think this corresponds to?

Badger Key Stage 4 Maths Starters

© Badger Publishing Ltd

Standard index notation

1 $342\,000 = 3.42 \times 10^5$

True or false?

2   Complete this statement:

54 670 = ...

3 $0.0029 = 2.9 \times 10^{-3}$

True or false?

4   Complete this statement:

0.00000519 = ...

Year 11 Maths Starter 17   **Number**

Reciprocals

Objective:

Understand the term reciprocal and use this in calculations involving powers.

Grade: A

What you will need:
OHT 17, class set of calculators.

Time:
5 minutes

Key words:

fraction, numerator, denominator, equivalent, reciprocal, product

Activity:

Show OHT 17. Give students 4-5 minutes to attempt the three problems in pairs.

Q: What did you make of these problems? What made the first one very easy to verify? How did it help when you then went on to attempt problem 2? What was the solution to problem 2?

What's the value of $\frac{2}{2}$? So, $\frac{2}{1} \times \frac{1}{2} = 1$. What do you notice? How did you solve the third problem? How could we use what we found in problem 2? How did we arrive at $\frac{2}{2}$ and that it's equivalent to 1? Give me another fraction that's equivalent to 1? What fraction could we multiply $\frac{3}{5}$ by to arrive at a fraction that's equivalent to 1? Why might we multiply the numerator by 5?

Links to plenary:

Q: Listen to this statement: '$\frac{5}{3}$ is the reciprocal of $\frac{3}{5}$.' Who can give me a definition of the word 'reciprocal'? What's the reciprocal of $\frac{7}{8}$? What happens when we multiply $\frac{7}{8}$ and $\frac{8}{7}$? Does the fact that the product is 1 help us to define the word 'reciprocal'?

Badger Key Stage 4 Maths Starters

© Badger Publishing Ltd

Year 11: Copymaster for Starter 17 (OHT)

Reciprocals

1. What is the value of $\frac{2}{1}$?

2. Find the value of $\frac{1}{2} \times \frac{2}{1}$

3. Find the missing fraction:

    $\frac{3}{5} \times ? = 1$

Badger Key Stage 4 Maths Starters

Year 11 Maths Starter 18 — Number

Irrational numbers

Objective:
Understand that pi and some roots are irrational; recognise that leaving solutions to problems in root form gives greater accuracy.

Grade: A

What you will need:
Class set of calculators.

Time:
5-10 minutes

Key words:
roots, value, pi, circumference, irrational numbers

Activity:

Ask the students:

Q: True or false: $\sqrt{2} \times \sqrt{3} = \sqrt{6}$? How can we test this statement? How might a calculator help us to test it?

Give students 1-2 minutes to discuss this in pairs.

Q: Was the statement true? Did the calculator confirm the statement? Did it come close to confirming it? Is that good enough? Why, when we know that the statement is true, does the calculator not give us exactly $\sqrt{6}$? What's special about these roots? How many decimal places do we have to go to before the digits in these roots, or the number pi, start to repeat themselves in a pattern? Will they ever repeat themselves? OK. We call numbers that behave in this way *irrational*. When might they be useful? True or false: the hypotenuse of a right-angle triangle with two shorter sides of 5 and 4 is 6.4?

Give students 1-2 minutes to discuss this in pairs.

Links to plenary:

Q: Is that the solution? Does it matter? If the dimensions I gave you were in cm? What if they were in metres? Kilometres? When might it be more appropriate to leave the solution in root form? Why?

Badger Key Stage 4 Maths Starters

© Badger Publishing Ltd

Year 11 Maths Starter 19   **Number**

Exponential growth and decay

Objective:
Understand exponential growth and decay, and use it to make predictions.

Grade: A/A*

What you will need:
OHT 19

Time:
5-10 minutes

Key words:
function, increase, decrease, variable, rate, value, axis, axes, plot, exponential, power, growth, decay

Activity:

Write, on the board, the function $y = 10^x$. Ask the students:

Q: How will this function behave? What do I mean by 'behave'? When x increases, will y increase? Will the two variables increase at the same rate? Which will increase faster? Will the rate at which y increases be much faster than the rate at which x increases? Why? What will happen when x is zero? When x becomes negative? What values of x will give us negative y values? Will y ever take a zero value? What drawing might help us to look at how the function behaves? What will the graph look like?

Show OHT 19.

Q: Why have we left off the values on the scales for the axes here? Are we going to sketch the graph or attempt to plot it? What problems will we encounter if we attempt to plot it? Would someone like to give me a co-ordinate that will be useful? Why might it be useful to plot the point where $x = 0$? Supposing I'd chosen the function $y = 15^x$. True or false: the graph would still pass through the point (0,1). Why?

With the students' help, sketch the basic exponential curve.

Links to plenary:

Q: Why might this curve be called a 'growth' curve? What might be growing? If we were charting the growth of a cell culture, for example, what would x represent in that context? Why might it be more sensible to plot y against t? What would the graph look like if we reflected it in the y axis? What name could we give that curve? What might be decaying?

Badger Key Stage 4 Maths Starters

© Badger Publishing Ltd

Year 11: Copymaster for Starter 19 (OHT)
Exponential growth and decay

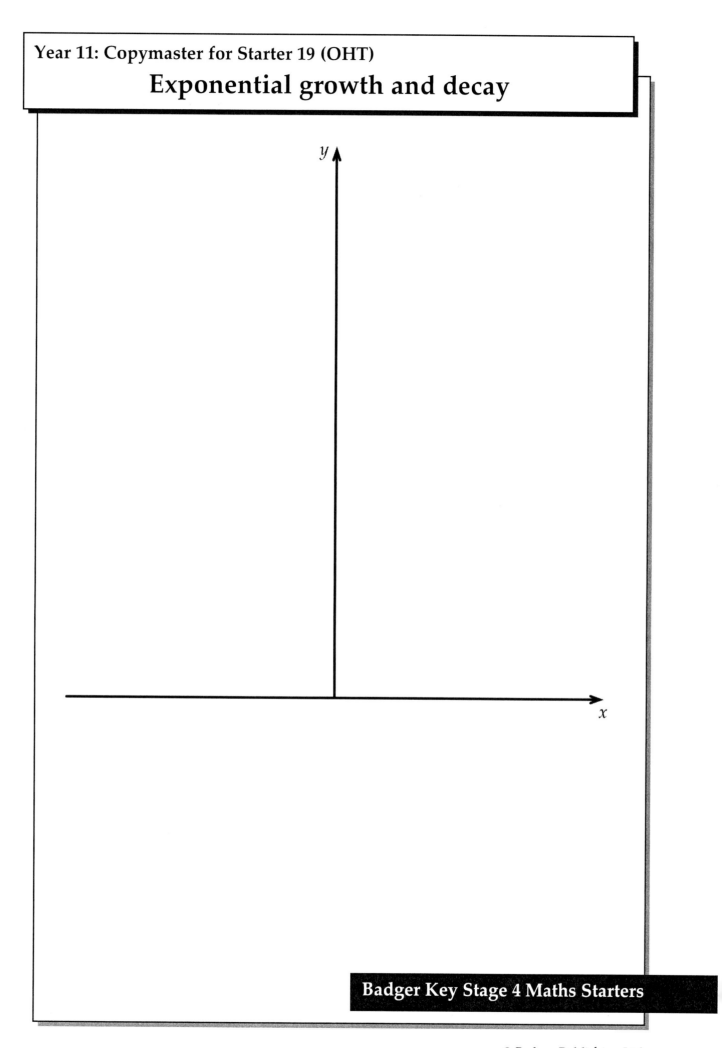

Badger Key Stage 4 Maths Starters

Year 11 Maths Starter 20 — Algebra
Substitute into expressions and formulae

Objective:

Substitute positive and negative values into expressions and formulae.

Grade: E/D

What you will need:
OHT 20

Time:
5-10 minutes

Key words:
  factor, prime, positive, integer, product

Activity:

Ask the students:

Q: What does this OHT show? Can we say more than 'algebra'? What kind of algebraic statements do we know? Is this an expression? How many variables are there in the statement? What do I mean by 'variable'? Does it show a relationship between the variables? What name do we give to this kind of statement? (Function) Does this function give us y in terms of x? What do I mean by that? Does y depend on x? How could we investigate this function? How could we see what happens to y as x changes? Can we choose x values to investigate? What's a simple x value to start with? If $x = 1$ (for example), how could we work out the corresponding value for y?

Give students 1-2 minutes to work out the y-value. (When $x = 1$, $y = 10.5$)

Q: How did you do it? Did anyone write out the function as a flow-chart? What happens to x first? Who squared x first? Who multiplied by 6 first? Does it matter? What did you do then?

Prompt students to substitute two or three more values into the expression - you might use the table on the OHT to record results. Students working at E/D level should substitute negative or decimal values.

Links to plenary:

Q: What problems did you encounter? Who tried −1? What did you notice? How does this function behave? What happened to y as x increased in size? Decreased? Do they both increase at the same rate? Which variable gets larger at a faster rate? What part of the function is making y increase at a greater rate? What might this look like on a graph?

Badger Key Stage 4 Maths Starters

© Badger Publishing Ltd

Year 10: Copymaster for Starter 20 (OHT)
Substitute into expressions and formulae

$$y = \frac{6x^2 + 15}{2}$$

x						
y						

Badger Key Stage 4 Maths Starters

© Badger Publishing Ltd

Year 11 Maths Starter 21

Algebra

Solve equations

Objective:
Balance equations, remove brackets in an equation and solve equations including examples where the unknown appears on both sides.

Grade: D

What you will need:
OHT 20

Time:
5-10 minutes

Key words:
unknown, expression, equation, value, solve, solution

Activity:

Show OHT 20, which shows the function investigated in the previous starter.

Ask the students:

Q: How could we work out the x value that gives a y value of 40.5? What different methods could we use? If we drew the graph of this function, could we read the value from the graph? Without the graph, could we use a trial-and-error method? How would we start? Can we set up an equation and solve it? Is this going to be a very challenging equation to solve? If so, why? Why does the divide by 2 part make it look challenging? Can we draw a flow-chart to help? How? What happens to x first? How could we work through the flow-chart backwards?

Give students 1-2 minutes to attempt to solve the equation. ($x = \sqrt{11}$)

Q: How did you do it? What inverses did you use? How did writing it out as a flow-chart help? Who used a balancing method? How did that work? Could we use this function to find a value for root 11? If we know that we must substitute root 11 in to get a y value of 40.5? What integer value for x is going to be close to root 11?

Links to plenary:

Q: If we substitute the value $x = 3$ into the function, do we get a y value close to 40.5? (It gives the value 34.5.) What x value should we try next? Why is it not sensible to try 4?

Badger Key Stage 4 Maths Starters

Year 11 Maths Starter 22

Algebra

Factorise

Objective:
Factorise with a constant term outside a single pair of brackets.

Grade: D

What you will need:
No additional resources.

Time:
5-10 minutes

Key words:
unknown, expression, function, factor, factorise, bracket, term

Activity:

Write, on the board, the equation $36 + 54 = 9(4 + 6)$. Ask the students:

Q: Is this statement true or false? What have I done to the left side to give the right side?

Give students 1-2 minutes to discuss these questions in pairs.

Q: Was it true? How did you test it? How did I devise the right-hand part of the equation? What key words could you use to explain? What did I notice about the numbers 36 and 54?

If they are both in the 9 times table, does that mean that 9 is a common factor? Once I spotted the common factor, what did I do then? How did I use the brackets? Why did I not include a 'multiply' sign? Do I need the brackets? OK. You try one. Factorise this expression:

Write on the board the expression: $21 - 49$. Give students 1-2 minutes to factorise.

Q: What did I mean by 'factorise'? How did you do it? What common factor did you spot? What did you do then? OK. Let's apply this skill to algebra.

Write on the board the expression: $16x + 28 = 4(4x + 7)$. Ask the students:

Q: Is this statement true or false? What have I done to the left side to give the right side?

Give students 1-2 minutes to discuss these questions in pairs.

Links to plenary:

Q: What did I do to factorise the algebraic expression? Once we identified 4 as a common factor, how did I divide $16x$ by 4? What did I do then? Do we need the brackets?

Badger Key Stage 4 Maths Starters

Year 11 Maths Starter 23   **Algebra**

Plot graphs

Objective:

Plot graphs using a table to generate points.

Grade: D

What you will need:
OHT 20 and OHT 23,
class set of worksheets.

Time:
5-10 minutes

Key words:
 function, graph, axis, axes, horizontal, vertical, scale

Activity:

Show OHT 20. Remind students that this is a function that they have met previously.

Q: Can you remember some of the pairs of values that we generated for this function? Did we find a value for y when x was zero? How? How could we find a value for x that makes y into zero? What happens if we turn it into an equation? Can we solve the equation to get an x value that makes y into zero? Why not? How could we use what we know about graphs to help us investigate this function? How could the pairs of values in the table help us? What kind of scale can be useful? Do we need to be able to plot negative y values? How does that help us when deciding on the scale to use?

Display OHT 23 and distribute the class set.

Q: Can someone remind me how we go about plotting our values on the graph?

Give students 3-4 minutes to plot the values as derived in a previous lesson.

Links to plenary:

Q: How did you do it? What values were easy to plot? Which were more difficult? Was it made easier by the fact that we'd worked out values in the previous lesson? What if I'd given you the function and asked you to plot the graph? What would have made it seem challenging? How can we remember the steps involved? Can we join the points? Can we join them to make a smooth curve? How can we use the graph to explain why we couldn't find x values that made y into zero?

Badger Key Stage 4 Maths Starters

© Badger Publishing Ltd

Year 11: Copymaster for Starter 23 (OHT)
Plot graphs

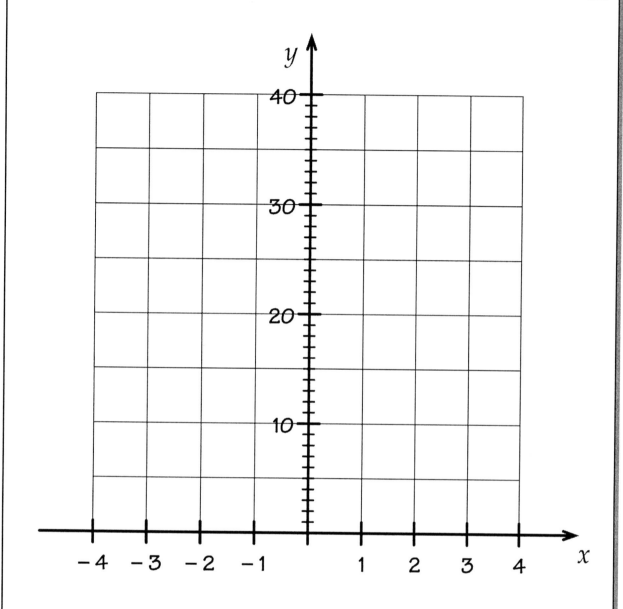

Badger Key Stage 4 Maths Starters

© Badger Publishing Ltd

Year 11 Maths Starter 24

Algebra

Real-life, distance/time and conversion graphs

Objective:
Read from real-life graphs, distance/time graphs and conversion graphs to solve problems; calculate speed from numerical data and from a graph.

Grade: D

What you will need:
OHT 24

Time:
5-10 minutes

Key words:
function, graph, axis, axes, horizontal, vertical, scale, unit, interpret

Activity:

Show OHT 24. Ask the students:

Q: What does this show? What does this graph represent? Is this the graph of a linear x, y function? How can you tell that it's not a simple function? Why is it not easy to interpret what the graph shows us? What's missing? What do you think the horizontal scale seems to represent? (Time) What other variable might be measured against time? Suppose the other variable was distance measured in km. Whose distance, from what? Does the graph show the movement of something or someone? Suppose the graph shows the movement of a person. Let's call the person Andrew. From what point might his movement be measured?

Prompt the students to decide on a starting point like a house or school.

Q: OK, so Andrew is moving from his house (for example). Can we tell at what times of the day Andrew was at his house? How can we identify these times? Does Andrew move away from his house? So his distance from the house increases. Does he come back to his house? Where on the graph is the point at which he begins to return?

Links to plenary:

Q: What is happening where the line is horizontal? Does it mean he's walking in a horizontal line? What could he be doing at 10.30? How far is he from his house? How can you tell? How far is he from his house at 10.31? 10.32? What's he doing? Where might he be? At what point is he moving most quickly? When is he walking more quickly ~ to the shop (for example) or when he's returning to his house? How can you tell?

Badger Key Stage 4 Maths Starters

© Badger Publishing Ltd

Year 11: Copymaster for Starter 24 (OHT)
Real-life, distance/time and conversion graphs

Badger Key Stage 4 Maths Starters

© Badger Publishing Ltd

Year 11 Maths Starter 25 — Algebra

Find the gradient and *y*-intercept

Objective:
From a given graph, find the gradient and *y*-intercept and hence the equation of the graph.

Grade: C/B

What you will need:
OHT 25

Time: 5-10 minutes

Key words:
percentage, increase, decrease, multiplier

Activity:
Show OHT 25.

Q: What does the OHT show? What kind of graphs are they? What different types of graph do we know? Are they conversion graphs? Do they show functions? What type of function? What different types of function do we know? Why might these be called linear functions? What did the person who drew these graphs have to begin with? What defined the relationship between *x* and *y* so that they could start to plot the points? Where did the points come from - how were they generated? OK. We are going to try and develop a method for finding the equations that they started with by investigating the graph. The equations for lines 1 and 2 are $y = 2x + 1$ and $y = 4x + 1$ respectively. What are the equations for lines 3 and 4?

Give students 1-2 minutes to discuss this question in pairs.

Q: What do you think the equations might be? How did you decide? What did you notice about the equations for lines 1 and 2? What was the same about them? How did this show itself on the graph? What was different? What effect did that have on the graph?

Links to plenary:
Q: How did you decide that lines 3 and 4 ended with −1? How did you decide that line 3 must be $y = 2x - 1$ and not, for example, $y = 5x - 1$? How did you use line 1 to help? What do you notice about lines 1 and 3? 2 and 4? How did the fact that they were parallel help? Do they have the same 'steepness'? Is there another word we can use for 'steepness'? How do we measure the gradient of a line?

Badger Key Stage 4 Maths Starters

© Badger Publishing Ltd

Year 11: Copymaster for Starter 25 (OHT)

Find the gradient and y-intercept

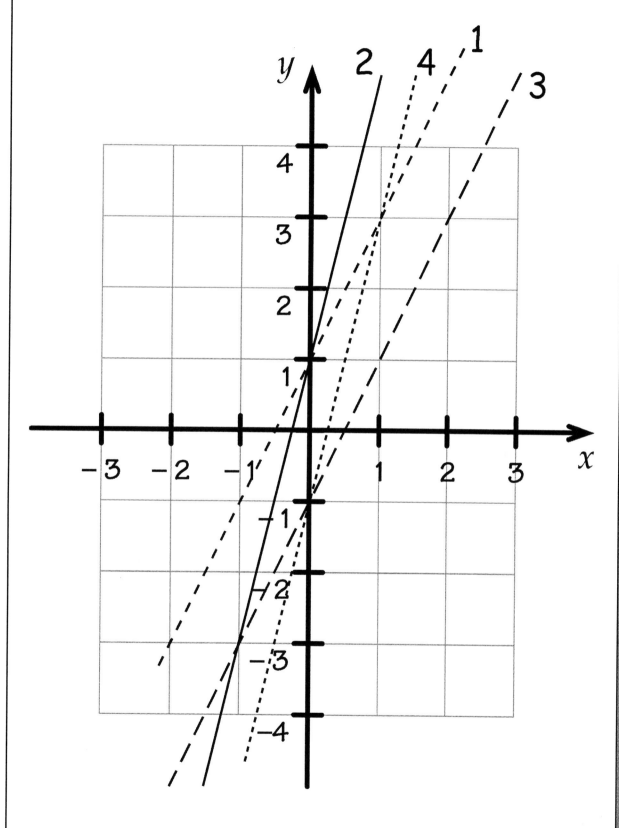

Badger Key Stage 4 Maths Starters

Year 11 Maths Starter 26 — Algebra

Draw a straight-line graph by using *m* and *c*

Objective:

Draw a straight-line graph without plotting points, i.e. by using *m* and *c*.

Grade: B

What you will need:
OHT 26, class set of worksheets.

Time:
5-10 minutes

Key words:
function, graph, plot, axis, axes, horizontal, vertical, scale, gradient, *y*-intercept

Activity:

Explain to the students:

This lesson is about using what we know about the gradient and the *y*-intercept to sketch a graph instead of plotting the graph.

Q: What do I mean by 'plotting' a graph? What do we need to plot a graph? What steps do we go through? What grade does being able to plot a graph correspond to? (D) Suppose we wanted, in our books, to draw a line that had a gradient of 1, how would we go about doing that?

Give students 1 minute to discuss this in pairs.

Q: How would we do it? If we count across and up, how many squares across do we go for every one square we go up? So we 'rise' 1 for every 1 we 'run'. Suppose we try a steeper line ~ with a gradient of 2. How many squares do we rise upwards for every one that we run across? Will that make the line steeper? Everyone draw a line with a gradient of 4. How did you do it?

Show OHT 26 and distribute class set. Prompt students to attempt to sketch the line $y = 3x + 2$. Give them 3-4 minutes to work in pairs.

Links to plenary:

Q: How did you do it? What did you need to decide first? What does the +2 on the equation tell us? What label do we give it? How is the *y*-intercept useful? Once we've put a cross at the *y*-intercept, what did you do then? How did you use the co-efficient of *x*? What do I mean by 'co-efficient'? What does the 3 tell us? How could we check that we've sketched it correctly? If we read a co-ordinate pair? What grade do you think sketching corresponds to? (B) Why do you think it's worth more than plotting?

Badger Key Stage 4 Maths Starters

Year 11: Copymaster for Starter 26 (OHT)

Draw a straight-line graph by using *m* and *c*

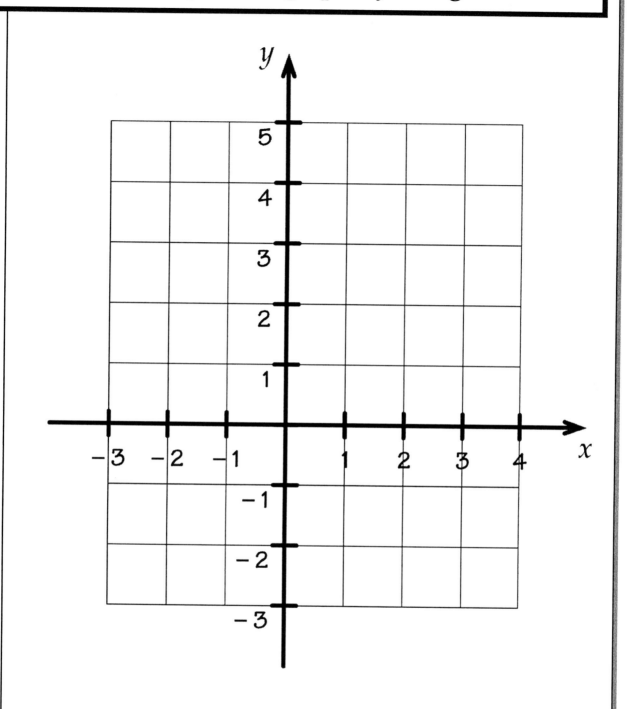

Badger Key Stage 4 Maths Starters

Year 11 Maths Starter 27 — Algebra
Expand and simplify linear expressions

Objective:
Expand and simplify pairs of linear expressions of the form $(x + p)(a + g)$.

Grade: B

What you will need:
No additional resources.

Time: 5-10 minutes

Key words:
linear expression, function, factor, factorise, bracket, term, expand, simplify

Activity:

Write on the board the equation: $(4 + 3)(5 + 7) = 20 + 28 + 15 + 21$. Ask the students:

Q: Is this statement true or false? What have I done to the left side to give the right side?

Give students 1-2 minutes to discuss these questions in pairs.

Q: Was it true? How did you test it? Where did the 20 come from? Where did the other values come from? Could I have multiplied the numbers in any other order? Is it useful to agree on an order so that we don't miss any values? How do we know that there must be four values? OK. Try one.

Write on the board the expression $(2 + 6)(8 - 5)$. Give students 1-2 minutes to expand this in pairs. Emphasise that it's the four vales you need to see ~ not the solution to the calculation.

Q: How did you do it? Did everyone do this in the same order? What effect did the subtraction have? Is this a particularly difficult skill? How might we apply it to a more complex aspect of mathematics?

Write on the board the expression $(x + 4)(x + 3)$. Give students 1-2 minutes to expand this in pairs.

Links to plenary:

Q: How did you do it? What happened when you multiplied x by itself? Which two terms did you multiply next? What do I mean by 'terms'? What four terms do we end up with? Can this be simplified? What grade do you think this skill corresponds to? How might we write a more challenging problem than the one we've just tried?

Badger Key Stage 4 Maths Starters

© Badger Publishing Ltd

Year 11 Maths Starter 28 Algebra

Factorise a quadratic

Objective:
Factorise a quadratic, e.g. $x^2 - 5x + 6 = (x - 6)(x + 1)$; use a factorised quadratic in one variable to solve a quadratic equation.

Grade: E

What you will need:
No additional resources.

Time:
5-10 minutes

Key words:
expression, function, factor, factorise, bracket, term

Activity:
Remind the students that they developed the ability to expand and simplify pairs of linear expressions of the form $(x + p)(a + g)$ in a previous lesson. They are now going to develop the reverse skill ~ beginning with an expanded expression.
Write the pair $(x + 2)(x + 6)$ on the board.

Q: Remind the students that they developed the ability to expand and simplify pairs of linear expressions of the form $(x + p)(a + g)$ in a previous lesson. They are now going to develop the reverse skill ~ beginning with an expanded expression. Write the pair $(x + 2)(x + 6)$ on the board.

Q: How might it help by rehearsing what we already know how to do? If we expand this expression, will it help us to then see how expressions can be factorised 'back into their brackets'? How?

Give students 3-4 minutes to discuss these questions in pairs, and then expand the expressions and consider how the resulting quadratic might be factorised.

Links to plenary:

Q: How might we factorise the quadratic if we didn't know what the pair of linear expressions that we began with were? How does the number 12 help us? Are 2 and 6 the only two numbers that multiply to give us 12? So what else did we need to look at? How did the 8 help? How could we practice this? Could we set the other problems in pairs? How could we make it more challenging? What effect would negatives have?

Badger Key Stage 4 Maths Starters

© Badger Publishing Ltd

Year 11 Maths Starter 29   Algebra

Plot quadratic and cubic curves

Objective:

Plot curves from given quadratic and cubic functions.

Grade: B/A

What you will need:
OHT 29, class set of worksheets.

Time:
5-10 minutes

Key words:
expression, function, linear function, quadratic, value, graph, axis, axes

Activity:

Write on the board the function $y = x^3$. Ask the students:

Q: What type of function is it? What different types of function do we know? Is this a linear function? Why might it be called a cubic function? How could we investigate the function to see how it behaves? Will it behave like a quadratic? As x increases, what happens to y? Does y increase at the same rate? What about when x decreases? Becomes negative? Can we predict the shape of the curve for this function? Can you agree on a sketch for the curve?

Give students 1-2 minutes to discuss this in pairs. Show OHT 29 and distribute class set.

Q: How can we test our prediction? What x values should we use? Why is there little point in going up to $x = 6$? What would the corresponding y value be?

Give students 4-5 minutes to plot the graph in pairs.

Links to plenary:

Q: How did you do it? What problems did you encounter? Does the graph go through the origin? What do I mean by 'origin'? What happens if we cube zero? What happens when we cube a negative number? Why will that give us a negative y value? How is this curve different to the $y = x^2$ curve?

Badger Key Stage 4 Maths Starters

© Badger Publishing Ltd

Year 11: Copymaster for Starter 29 (OHT)
Plot quadratic and cubic curves

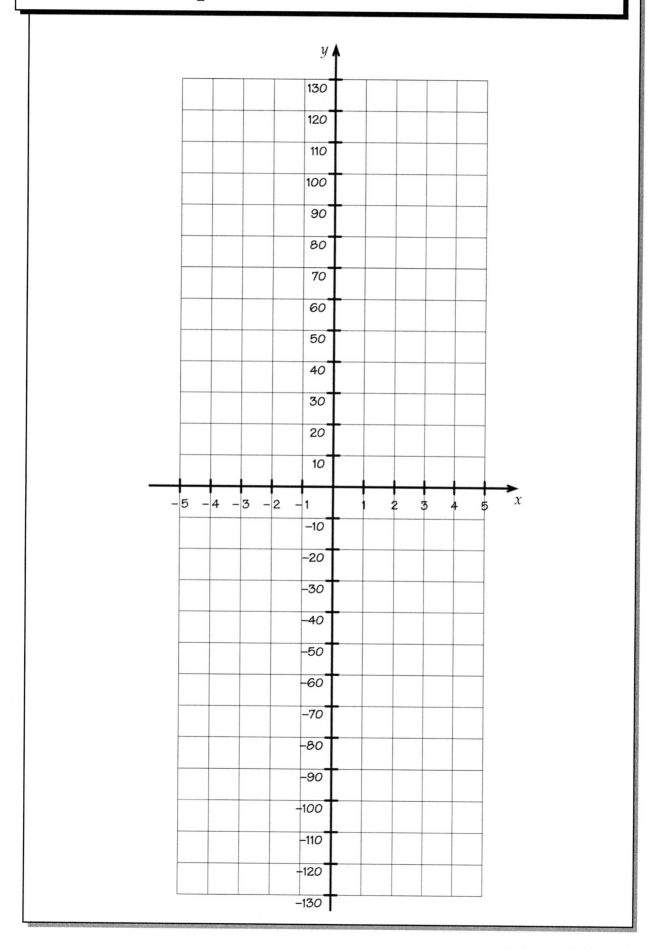

© Badger Publishing Ltd

Year 11 Maths Starter 30 — Algebra
Solve quadratics

Objective:

Solve quadratic equations by factorisation.

Grade: B/A

What you will need:
OHT 30

Time:
5-10 minutes

Key words:

expression, function, equation, quadratic, factorise, solve, root

Activity:

Write on the board the quadratic equation $x^2 - 5x + 6 = 0$. Prompt students to solve it. Give them 1-2 minutes.

Q: Did anyone try to use a balancing method? Did you arrive at $x^2 - 5x = -6$? What did you do then? Did you try to use a trial-and-error method? Why is this not an efficient way of attempting to solve the equation? If I'd left off the '= 0' part, what problem could I have set with the quadratic on its own? Could this have been a 'factorise' problem? Might factorising the equation help?

Give students 1-2 minutes to factorise the equation. Show OHT 30.

Q: What's the value of a in the first equation? The value of b in the second? What could the values of a and b be in the third? Must at least one of them be zero? Can we write that either $a = 0$ or $b = 0$? OK. The third equation is the factorised form of the quadratic we began with. Do we have an equation in which one 'thing', $(x - 2)$, multiplied by another 'thing', $(x - 3)$, gives zero? Does at least one of these 'things' have to be zero for that to be true? Finish the statement: 'Either $x - 2 = 0$...' What two values can x be? How do we complete the solution?

Links to plenary:

Q: How could we test the values we've derived? If we substitute the value $x = 2$ into the expression $x^2 - 5x + 6$, what value will the expression take? What if we substitute the value $x = 3$ into the expression? How could we use these values? How might they help us to sketch the curve $y = x^2 - 5x + 6$?

Badger Key Stage 4 Maths Starters

Year 11: Copymaster for Starter 30 (OHT)

Solve quadratics

1 $a \times 8 = 0$

2 $12 \times b = 0$

3 $a \times b = 0$

4 $(x - 2)(x - 3) = 0$

Badger Key Stage 4 Maths Starters

Year 11 Maths Starter 31 — Algebra

The difference of two squares

Objective:

Factorise using the difference of two squares and use this to solve problems.

Grade: B / A

What you will need:
No additional resources.

Time:
5-10 minutes

Key words:

expression, function, equation, quadratic, factorise, expand, term

Activity:

Write on the board the equation: $x^2 - 9 = (x + 3)(x - 3)$. Ask the students:

Q: Is this statement true or false? What have I done to the left side to give the right side?

Give students 1-2 minutes to discuss these questions in pairs.

Q: Was it true? How did you test it? Why does $(x + 3)(x - 3)$ expand to an expression with no x term? Where does it go? Why does this happen? How do the two constant terms in the pair ensure that the x term cancels out? Can we devise another pair of linear equations that will expand to give a quadratic with no x term?

Give students 1-2 minutes to find another pair.

Q: What did you come up with? Why might these types of quadratics be referred to as the difference between two squares?

Write on the board the equation $45^2 - 43^2 = (45 + 43)(45 - 43)$.

Q: True or false? How can we test? What's $45 + 43$? Multiplied by $45 - 43$? OK. Find the value of $17.5^2 - 11.5^2$.

Links to plenary:

Q: How did you do it? What other problems could we set to test this skill? What grade do you think this skill corresponds to? What makes it worth the B grade?

Badger Key Stage 4 Maths Starters

Year 11 Maths Starter 32
Simplify algebraic fractions
Algebra

Objective:

Add and simplify algebraic fractions.

Grade: B/A

What you will need:
OHT 32

Time:
5-10 minutes

Key words:

expression, unknown, simplify, denominator, numerator

Activity:

Show OHT 32. Ask the students to discuss how they might simplify the two fractions, resolving them into a single fraction by addition. Give them 3-4 minutes to attempt this.

Q: How did you get on? What makes this look challenging? What grade do you think this corresponds to? Is it impossible for us to begin to simplify this? What type of expressions are these? If there were no unknown letter symbols, just numbers, what would we call these? Are they fractions? What do we know about the addition of fractions? Can we use any of what we know about fractions to help us? How would we add the fraction $\frac{3}{4}$ and $\frac{2}{5}$? Why are they not easy to add simply? What do we have to find? What is the common denominator? How did you find it? What do we multiply 4 by? What do we multiply 5 by? So we multiply each by the other? Can we try the same approach for the algebraic fractions? What shall we multiply the x by? The y by? Do we only multiply the denominators? So by what are we multiplying the 8? The $2x$? What two fractions does that give us? Can we now add the two fractions? What will that give us?

Prompt the students to attempt the second problem on the OHT. Give them 2-3 minutes.

Links to plenary:

Q: How did you do it? In what ways was it different to the first problem? How did it simplify? Have we now learned this new skill? Do we need to practice it? What grade do you think this skill corresponds to? Could we devise a more challenging problem?

Badger Key Stage 4 Maths Starters

© Badger Publishing Ltd

Year 11: Copymaster for Starter 32 (OHT)

Simplify algebraic fractions

1 $\quad \dfrac{8}{x} + \dfrac{2x}{y}$

2 $\quad \dfrac{7a}{5} - \dfrac{10}{a}$

Year 11 Maths Starter 33

Algebra

Solve simultaneous equations

Objective:

Solve simultaneous equations by eliminating a variable.

Grade: C

What you will need:
No additional resources.

Time:
5-10 minutes

Key words:
equation, expression, unknown, value, variable, solve

Activity:

Explain to the students that you have thought of two integers, x and y. (8 and 3) You are not going to reveal their values. But when you add them together they give 11. And if you double x and then add y it gives 19. Prompt them to work out the two values. Give them 2 minutes.

Q: How did you do it? What did you write down as I read out the information? Did anyone write these as equations? What did you write? In what ways was the second equation different to the first? What extra thing did it have? Was that the only difference? So what effect did that extra x have on the value of the second equation? Was it that one extra x that increased the value from 11 to 19? How can we use that thought to find the value of x? How could we now work out the value of y? How could we test our values? Can we devise similar problems for each other to practice this new skill?

Give students 3-4 minutes to set and solve each other's problem in pairs.

Links to plenary:

Q: Did anyone devise problems that were more challenging than the one we began with? How could we make more challenging problems? How might throwing in a subtraction make the problem more challenging? How could we adapt our method to solve this more challenging type of problem?

Badger Key Stage 4 Maths Starters

© Badger Publishing Ltd

Year 11 Maths Starter 34
Algebra

Linear inequalities

Objective:
Solve linear inequalities through algebraic methods; list possible integer values for given inequalities.

Grade: C

What you will need:
OHT 34

Time:
5-10 minutes

Key words:
equation, inequality, expression, unknown, value, larger than, less than, less than or equal to, larger than or equal to

Activity:
Ask the students:

Q: I've thought of an integer, x. What values could x take? How many different values are possible? How could I impose limits on x so that there aren't an infinite number of possible values? If I give you a lower limit, will there still be an infinite number of possible values? OK. x must be larger than -2 and less than 7. How many different values are possible? What are they?

Model listing all the integer values on the board: (-1, 0, 1, 2, 3, 4, 5, 6)

Q: Why did we not include -2 or 7? How could I have changed the way I defined the upper limit so that we did include 7? What if I'm not allowed to use the word 'eight'? What symbols do we use to say that one value is less than another? Less than or equal to?

Show OHT 34. Ask the students:

Q: How could we show on this number line all the possible values that satisfy this inequality? What do you think I mean by 'inequality'?

Links to plenary:
Q: Imagine a builder is going to buy 2 bags of sand. He needs at least 100kg of sand. His van can take a maximum load of 350kg. He must choose two bags. What's the smallest bag that he can choose **two** of? The heaviest?

Badger Key Stage 4 Maths Starters

Year 11: Copymaster for Starter 34 (OHT)
Linear inequalities

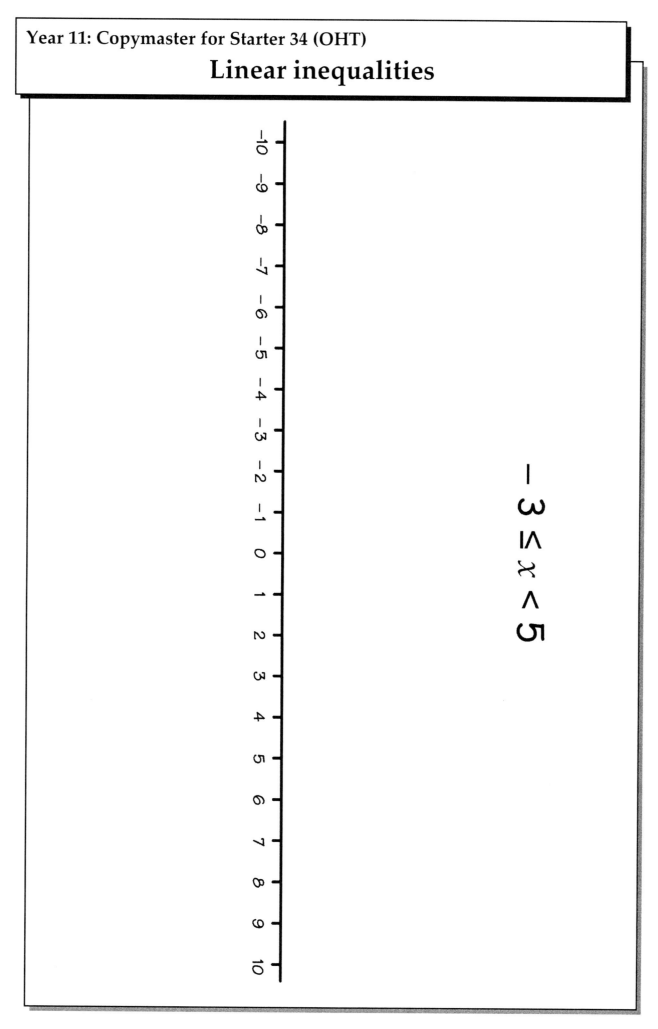

$-3 \leq x < 5$

© Badger Publishing Ltd

Year 11 Maths Starter 35 — Algebra

The curves $y = \sin x$, $y = \cos x$ and $y = \tan x$

Objective:

Sketch the curves $y = \sin x$, $y = \cos x$ and $y = \tan x$.

Grade: A/A*

What you will need:
OHT 35, class set of worksheets, class set of calculators.

Time:
10 minutes

Key words:
graph, axis, axes, sin, cos, tan, plot, curve, right-angled triangle, hypotenuse, opposite, adjacent

Activity:

Show OHT 35 and distribute class set. Ask the students:

Q: What do you notice about the scales for these axes? What's unusual about the way in which the x axis has been calibrated? What 'key' values is x taking? What could x represent here? What function could we show that involves angles? How could we plot the graph of $y = \sin x$? What equipment do we need? What values should we start with for x? What is $\sin 0°$? What other values should we calculate?

Give students 2-3 minutes to calculate and plot values in pairs.

Q: What did you notice about the values? How would you describe the way that they repeat themselves? Why do you think the value of $\sin 90°$ is 1? (Refer to the right-angled triangle on the OHT.) If sin is the ratio of opposite/hypotenuse, which side is opposite the 90° angle? How should we join the points? With straight lines? Curves? How can we decide? Why might the value of $\sin 89°$ help? $\sin 91°$? What other values might help? What other graphs could we explore?

Links to plenary:

Q: Can we predict the shape of the graph of $y = \cos x$? $y = \tan x$? What's the value of $\tan 90°$? Why is there no value? (Refer again to the right-angled triangle on the OHT.) What side is opposite the 90° angle? Adjacent? Does it have an adjacent? How can we explore what the graph does around the impossible value $\tan 90°$?

Badger Key Stage 4 Maths Starters

© Badger Publishing Ltd

Year 11: Copymaster for Starter 35 (OHT)
The curves $y = \sin x$, $y = \cos x$ and $y = \tan x$

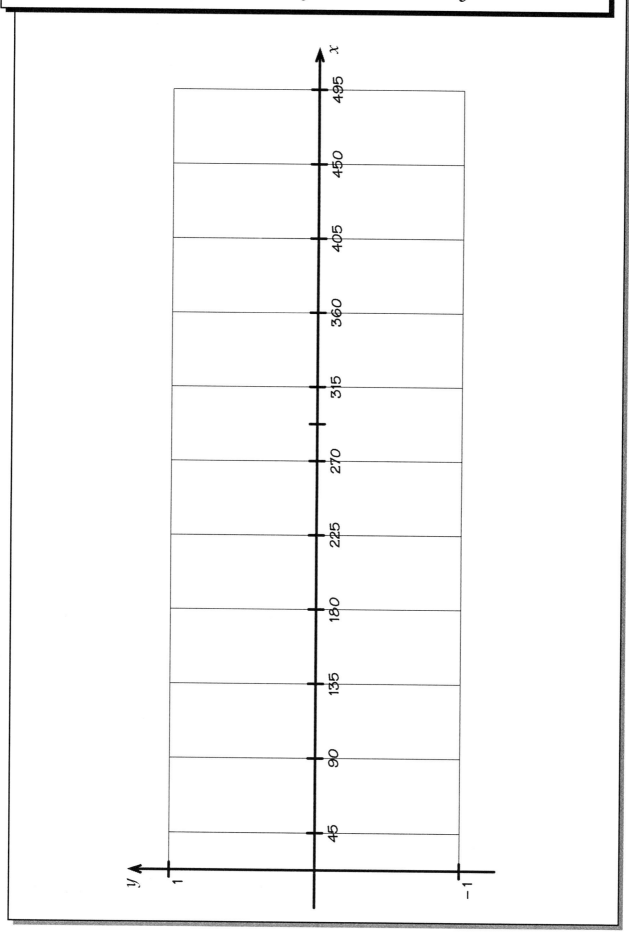

Year 11 Maths Starter 36	Algebra

Graphs such as $y = a + b \sin x$

Objective:

Sketch such graphs as $y = a + b \sin x$.

Grade: A*

What you will need:
OHT 35, class set of worksheets, class set of calculators.

Time:
10 minutes

Key words:

graph, axis, axes, sin, cos, tan, plot, curve, right-angled triangle, hypotenuse, opposite, adjacent, trigonometry, constant, translate

Activity:

Explain to the students that they are going to explore what happens to the trig functions if we add a constant to them.

Q: What do I mean by 'add a constant'? Are constants the opposite of variables? What constants could we choose? What effect do you think adding 2 to the value of sin x will have on the shape of the sin curve? Will it stretch the curve? Will it transform or translate it in some way? What do I mean by 'translate'? What's the value of 2 + sin 90°? How did you work it out without the calculator? Are there 'key' values for the trig functions that we should remember?

Show OHT 35, from the previous starter, and distribute class set. Give students 3-4 minutes to calculate values for $y = 2 + \sin x$ in pairs.

Q: How did you get on? Can you describe the effect that adding 2 to the values had on the curve? Can we use the key words? In which direction was the curve translated?

Links to plenary:

Q: What effect would adding the constant to the angle and then finding the trig function of the angle have? What do I mean? Suppose we add the constant 10° to each angle and then find the sin of that value. How would we write that as a function? What's sin 90°? What's sin 90° + 10°? Can you predict how adding this constant will affect the curve?

Badger Key Stage 4 Maths Starters

Year 11 Maths Starter 37

Algebra

The graphs of $y = f(x) + a$, $y = f(ax)$, $y = f(x + a)$, and $y = af(x)$

Objective:

Given the graph of $y = f(x)$, be able to sketch the graphs of $y = f(x) + a$, $y = f(ax)$, $y = f(x + a)$, and $y = af(x)$ by applying transformations (for linear, quadratic, sine and cosine functions).

Grade: A/A*

What you will need:
OHT 37

Time: 10 minutes

Key words: function, graph, axis, axes, horizontal, vertical, parabola, scale, linear function, quadratic, $y = f(x)$, curve

Activity:

Write on the board the statement: $y = f(x)$. Ask the students:

Q: What could this mean? What might the f stand for? If it stood for 'function', what would 'y equals function x' mean? Why might this notation be useful?

Show OHT 37.

Q: What function is shown here? ($y = x^2$) What shape does the function give? How could I use the function notation to show the equation which gives this graph? Suppose this is the graph of $f(x)$ and that $f(x) = x^2$. What would the graph of $f(x) + 1$ look like?

Give students 1-2 minutes to discuss this in pairs.

Q: Can we predict what adding 1 to the function will do to the curve? How could we test the prediction? If x is 1, what's the value of $f(x)$? Where is that on the graph? What would the value of $f(x) + 1$ be? Where is that on the graph? Can we begin to see what's happening? Can we use the word 'translate' to describe what's happening? Can we predict what the graph of $f(x + 1)$ will be?

Give students 1-2 minutes to discuss this in pairs.

Links to plenary:

Q: Will this be the same as $f(x) + 1$? At what point when calculating the values to plot would we add 1? If $x = -1$, what would $x + 1$ be? And then square it? So instead of the co-ordinate being $(-1, 1)$ (for $f(x) = x^2$) it would be $(1, 0)$. When $x = 0$, what will the value of $f(x + 1)$ be? If $x = 1$? Can you describe what translation has been applied to the $f(x) = x^2$ curve to give the $f(x + 1)$ curve? How could we generalise these results?

Badger Key Stage 4 Maths Starters

© Badger Publishing Ltd

Year 11: Copymaster for Starter 37 (OHT)

The graphs of $y = f(x) + a$, $y = f(ax)$, $y = f(x + a)$, and $y = af(x)$

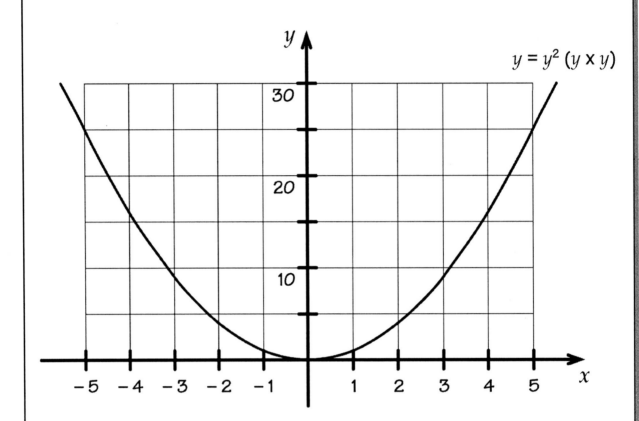

$y = y^2$ ($y \times y$)

Badger Key Stage 4 Maths Starters

Year 11 Maths Starter 38 — Algebra

Express a circle in algebraic form

Objective:

Express a circle of radius r, and centre $(0,0)$ in algebraic form.

Grade: A/A*

What you will need:
OHT 38, class set of worksheets.

Time:
5-10 minutes

Key words:
origin, radius, function, circle, Pythagoras' theorem, hypotenuse

Activity:

Write, on the board, the equation $x^2 + y^2 = 25$. Ask the students:

Q: Can someone suggest values for x and y that will make this true? Which pair of integer values will make this true? (3 and 4)

Show OHT 38. Plot the co-ordinate (3, 4).

Q: What will the distance from the origin to this point be? (5) Why? What other integer pairs work? Could x be –3? And y? Could one be positive and the other negative? Could x be 4 and y be 3? Could they also be negative?

Plot co-ordinates (3, –4), (–3, –4,), (–3, 4), (4, 3), (–4, 3) etc on the OHT.

Q: What will the distances from the origin to these points be? Will (5, 0) work? (0, 5)? If we continued to plot pairs of values that satisfy this equation, what shape will they describe? How could we find non-integer values for x and y? Can we choose a value for x and then work out the corresponding value for y?

Give students 3-4 minutes to calculate non-linear values and plot the circle on their worksheets.

Links to plenary:

Q: How could we generalise this result? What do I mean by 'generalise'? Are we saying that graphs of the form $x^2 + y^2 = 25$ will always give us a circle? Can you give me another equation of the form $x^2 + y^2 = 25$? What about $x^2 + y^2 = 16$? Where would the centre of the circle be? What key word can we use? What will the radius of the circle be? Suppose I wanted to draw a circle with a radius of 8 units? What equation would we use? What if I wanted to draw a circle, radius r?

Badger Key Stage 4 Maths Starters

© Badger Publishing Ltd

Year 11: Copymaster for Starter 38 (OHT)

Express a circle in algebraic form

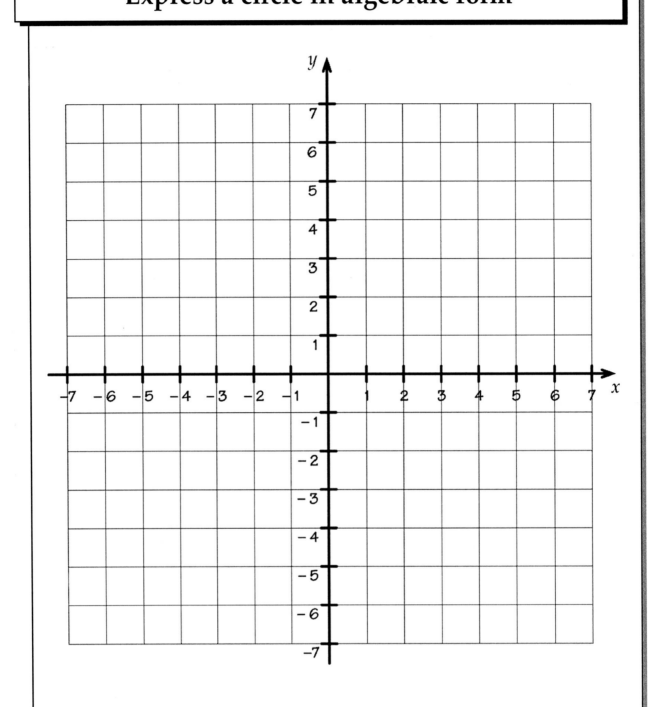

Badger Key Stage 4 Maths Starters

© Badger Publishing Ltd

Year 11 Maths Starter 39 — **Algebra**

Solve a pair of simultaneous equations (one non-linear)

Objective:

Solve by substitution a pair of simultaneous equations (one non-linear).

Grade: A/A*

What you will need:
No additional resources.

Time:
5-10 minutes

Key words:

function, graph, axis, axes, quadratic, parabola, simultaneous equation, solve, factorise

Activity:

Write on the board the two equations $y = x + 2$ and $y = x^2 + 2x - 3$. Ask the students:

Q: How could we find the co-ordinates of the point or points at which the graphs of these two will intersect? Why might there be more than one point? Can we treat the two as simultaneous equations? How might we solve them?

Give students 2-3 minutes to discuss this in pairs.

Q: Can we solve them by elimination? What do I mean by 'elimination'? What do we have to do first? How will we rearrange the equations? What will that give us? Do we add or subtract the equations to eliminate y? Talk me through how we eliminate y. What type of equation do we then have? What should we do now? Will the quadratic factorise easily? What should we do next? Can we remember the quadratic formula?

Give students 2-3 minutes to factorise the quadratic ($x^2 + x - 5 = 0$).

Links to plenary:

Q: How did you find the roots of the equation? Have we finished? Have we solved the problem? What have we found so far? Can we say where the two graphs intersect? Into which equations do we substitute the two values for x to find corresponding values for y?

Badger Key Stage 4 Maths Starters

© Badger Publishing Ltd

Year 11 Maths Starter 40 Algebra
Calculate where a straight-line graph meets a circle

Objective:
Use simultaneous equations to calculate where a straight-line graph meets a circle.

Grade: A*

What you will need:
No additional resources.

Time:
10 minutes

Key words:
function, graph, axis, axes, origin, quadratic, simultaneous equation, solve, factorise

Activity:

Ask the students:

Q: Give me an example of a linear equation. A quadratic? Give me an example of an equation that will give a circle with the origin as its centre. OK. This starter is about finding intersection points between a circle and a straight line. The aim is to calculate where the line $y = 2x - 1$ meets the circle given by $x^2 + y^2 = 4$. Will there be one point or must there, by definition, be two? Can a line merely touch the circle? OK. Will these lines meet twice? I want you to decide how we are going to find the points at which the two graphs meet.

Give students 2-3 minutes to discuss this in pairs.

Q: What are we going to do? Will drawing the graphs help? If the co-ordinates are integer co-ordinates? What if they aren't? Will the graph give us accurate readings? Are we looking at two simultaneous equations? What method of solution should we use? What methods are there? Why might substitution be an appropriate method? What are we going to substitute into what? If we substitute $2x - 1$ for y in $x^2 + y^2 = 4$, what kind of equation will we derive? What will we do then?

Give students 4-5 minutes to find the roots for the resulting quadratic.

Links to plenary:

Q: How did you do it? How did you substitute $2x - 1$ for y into $x^2 + y^2 = 4$? Did that involve an expansion? What did you do next? How did it simplify? Were you then looking for the roots of the quadratic? How did you find them? What were the roots? (2.18 and –13.78.) Have we completed the problem? What else must we do? Have we the co-ordinates of the two points where the graphs meet?

Badger Key Stage 4 Maths Starters

© Badger Publishing Ltd

Year 11 Maths Starter 41 *Shape, space and measures*

Translate simple 2D shapes

Objective:
Recognise translations as sliding movements and translate simple 2D shapes within a plane.

Grade: F/E

What you will need:
OHT 41

Time:
5 minutes

Key words:
2D shape, congruent, axis, axes, vertical, horizontal, transform, translate, vertex, vertices

Activity:
Ask the students:

Q: In what different ways can we *transform* a 2D shape? What do I mean by 'transform'? What things can we do to change a shape? If we reflect a shape, what things about the shape will change? Will it still have the same dimensions? Interior angles? What will change? What about if we rotate a shape? What will change? What other transformations do we know? Is enlargement a type of transformation? What changes when we enlarge a shape?

Show OHT 41. Ask the students:

Q: What do you think we are being asked to do here? What do you think 'translate' means in this question? When do we normally meet the word 'translate'? What does it mean in that context? Can we translate a shape? Can you give me another word for translate in this question? Could 'move' be that other word?

Links to plenary:

Q: How can we solve the problem on the OHT? Should we try to translate the whole shape in one go? Why might it be more sensible to translate a side or a vertex first? What do I mean by 'vertex'? Should we do it vertex by vertex? How?

Translate the shape by following the students' oral instructions.

Badger Key Stage 4 Maths Starters

© Badger Publishing Ltd

Year 11: Copymaster for Starter 41 (OHT)

Translate simple 2D shapes

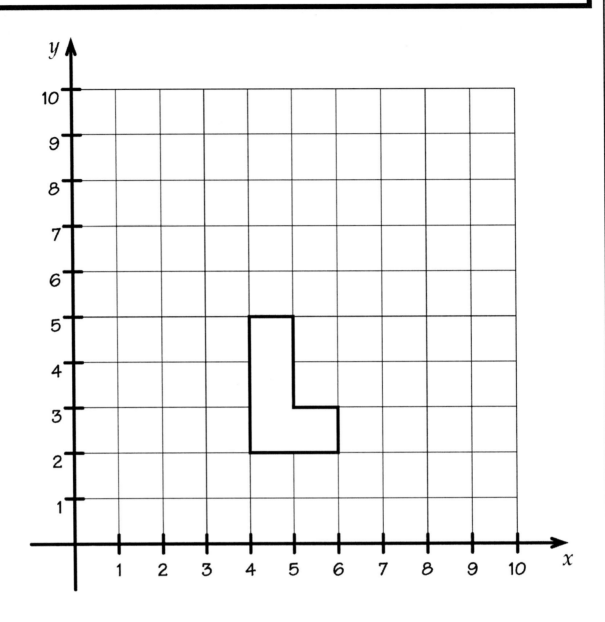

Translate this shape −2 squares across, 5 squares up.

Badger Key Stage 4 Maths Starters

Year 11 Maths Starter 42　　　　　　　　*Shape, space and measures*

Corresponding and alternate angles

Objective:

Recognise and solve problems involving corresponding and alternate angles.

Grade: D

What you will need:
OHT 42

Time:
5-10 minutes

Key words: parallel, transversal, angle, opposite angle, angles on a straight line, corresponding angle, alternate angle

Activity:

Show OHT 42. Refer to problem 1. Give the students 1-2 minutes to read it.

Q: Will Brian finish the job? How can you tell? What made it into a problem that needed working through? Did the fact that the statements aren't in the right order make it slightly difficult? How did you unpick the problem? Did it help to put them into a more logical order? What do I mean by 'logical'?

Refer to problem 2.

Q: How can we use what we've just done to solve this problem? Is there any similarity between the two problems at all? How can there be if problem 1 is a series of statements and problem 2 is a diagram? Can we write any statements about the angles in the diagram? What angle facts will we need to remember? Can we choose angles in any order and then put them in order when we've written the statements? What might the first angle fact be? Why might it be useful to focus on angle b first? What statement could we write for b? Finish the statement: 'Angle b is 55° because…' Now that we've shown that b is 55°, what angle should we go to next?

Give students 3-4 minutes, working in pairs, to solve the problem.

Links to plenary:

Q: How did you show that angle c must be 55° as well? What angle fact did you use? What did you do then? What angle fact justifies the statement that angle a must be 125°? Was there another, shorter way of showing that angle a must be 125°? Do we need to refer to b at all? What other angle fact tells us that c must be 55°? Will we need to recognise alternate and corresponding angles in our everyday lives? So what is this on the curriculum for? Is the logical thinking behind it the skill that we may find useful?

Badger Key Stage 4 Maths Starters

© Badger Publishing Ltd

Corresponding and alternate angles

Problem 1: Will Brian finish the job?

If Brian gets the paper, he can finish the job.
Alan remembers.
If Jane is driven to work, she'll get there early.
If Alan remembers, he will drive Jane to work.
If Jane gets to work early, she can give the paper to Brian.

Problem 2: Show that angle $a = 125°$.

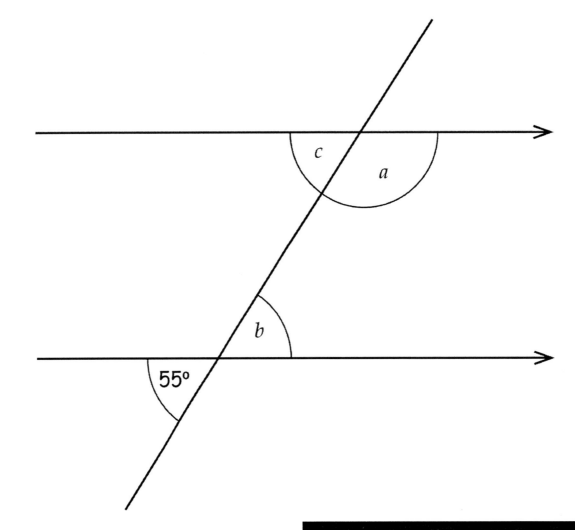

Year 11 Maths Starter 43 — Shape, space and measures

Properties of a parallelogram

Objective:
Use parallel line properties of a parallelogram or rhombus to solve problems.
Grade: D

What you will need:
OHT 43

Time:
5-10 minutes

Key words:
parallel, parallelogram, transversal, angle, opposite angle, angles on a straight line, corresponding angle, alternate angle

Activity:

Show OHT 43. Ask the students:

Q: What angle facts will help us with this problem? Is there a shape in the diagram? What properties of the parallelogram might help us? What do I mean by 'properties'? What are the properties of the parallelogram? OK. What's the first angle fact that we can write down? Why might it be sensible to focus our attention on angle r first? What angle fact are we going to use? What angle fact are we going to show next? How might the properties of the parallelogram help us?

Give students 3-4 minutes, working in pairs, to solve the problem.

Links to plenary:

Q: What use did you make of one of the properties of the parallelogram? What can we say about angles q and r? What fact proves that they are equal? What did you do then? Have we finished the problem? What fact do we use to justify the statement that $p = 114°$? What grade do you think this corresponds to? What makes it a D grade problem? What might make it challenging in an exam situation? How do we remember the angle facts that we need?

Badger Key Stage 4 Maths Starters

Year 11: Copymaster for Starter 43 (OHT)

Properties of a parallelogram

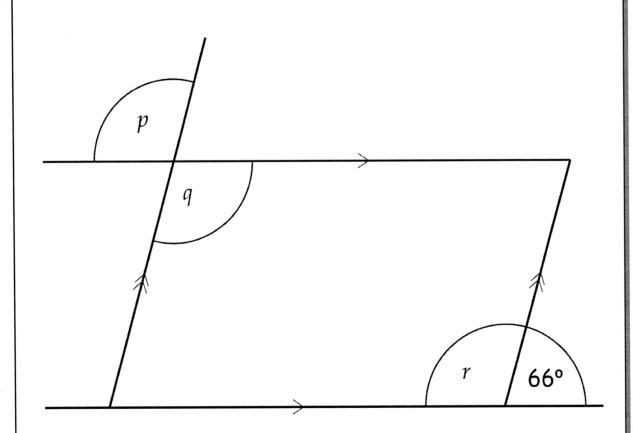

Show that $p = 114°$

Year 11 Maths Starter 44
Triangle proofs

Shape, space and measures

Objective:
Understand proof that angles in a triangle sum to 180° and that an exterior angle is equal to the sum of the two opposite interior angles.

Grade: D/C

What you will need:
OHT 44

Time: 10 minutes

Key words:
parallel, transversal, angle, opposite angle, angles on a straight line, corresponding angle, alternate angle, triangle, interior angles

Activity:

Show OHT 44. Refer to the first set of statements.

Q: What can we say about the sum of c and d? How do all these statements lead us to the conclusion that $c + d$ must equal z? Is there a logic to the statements? Do we need *all* of the statements or could we show that $c + d = z$ without one of the statements? What do you think of the way that the words 'but', 'and' and 'so' have been used to link the statements? How could we use this thinking to *prove* that the angles of the triangle sum to 180°?

Give students 2-3 minutes, working in pairs, to examine the diagram on the OHT and consider how they might construct a proof.

Q: Suppose we don't know that the interior angles of the triangle sum to 180°. We suspect that they do. We do know that the angles on a straight line sum to 180° and that alternate angles are equal. We have those facts ~ someone else has proved them beyond all doubt and given them to us. What statements could we write about some of the angles in the diagram? Could we use algebra to write statements? Is it true to say that $a + p + b$ must sum to 180°? What angle fact proves this? So $a + p + b = 180°$. What next? Could we start the next statement with the word 'but'? How would we continue our proof?

Links to plenary:

Q: How are we going to make the link between the angles a, p and b on a straight line and the interior angles of the triangle? What angle fact are we going to use to justify our statements? If we write that $q = a$ and $r = b$, are we close to concluding our proof?

Refer to the second diagram on the OHT.

Q: How could we use this diagram to prove that the exterior angle of the triangle is equal to the sum of the two opposite interior angles?

Badger Key Stage 4 Maths Starters

© Badger Publishing Ltd

Triangle proofs

$a + b = z$
but $c = a$
and $d = b$
so $c + d = ?$

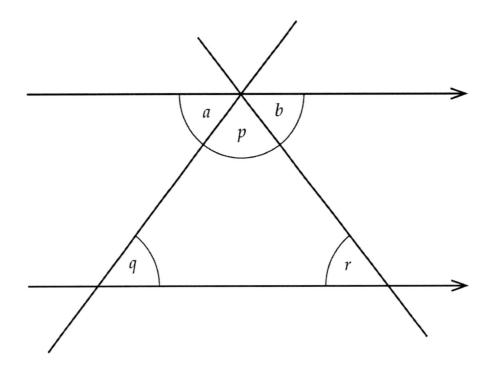

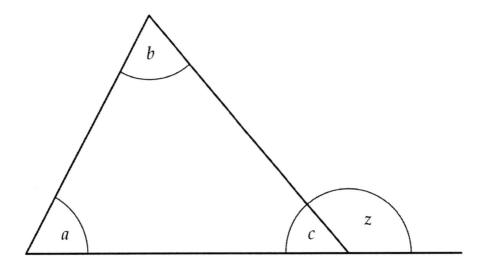

Year 11 Maths Starter 45 — *Shape, space and measures*

Describe solid shapes

Objective:

Describe solid shapes in terms of edges, vertices and faces.

Grade: E/D

What you will need:
OHT 45

Time:
5-10 minutes

Key words:
3D shape, solid, surface area, net, cube, cuboid, prism, face, edge, vertex, vertices

Activity:

Show OHT 45. Refer to the cuboid diagram.

Q: What name do we give this solid? What do I mean by 'solid'? How many faces does it have? What do I mean by 'face'? What shape are each of the six faces? Are they six differently shaped rectangles? How many edges does the solid have? What do I mean by 'edges'? Can we define an edge as the line where two faces meet? What name do we give to the point where three edges meet? If one is called a vertex, what word do we use for several? How many vertices does the cuboid have? Which face on the cuboid is shaded?

Give students 1 minute to discuss how they might refer to the shaded face.

Q: What labels could we give it? If we decide to call it the 'upper' face, what names could we give the other faces? What edge has been shown with 'blobs' on it? Why is it difficult to refer to the edges? What system can we impose on the diagram to make it easier to refer to faces, edges and vertices?

Give students 1-2 minutes to discuss this.

Links to plenary:

Q: What system do we use when labelling lines or 2D shapes? Can we use letters to label the solid? Where should we put the letters? Should we give every face a letter? Every edge? Every vertex? Is there a simpler way? If we put letters at each vertex, how could we use them to refer to one of the edges? (Label the vertices on the OHT with capital letters.) Which edge has 'blobs'? Which face is shaded?

Badger Key Stage 4 Maths Starters

Year 11: Copymaster for Starter 45 (OHT)
Describe solid shapes

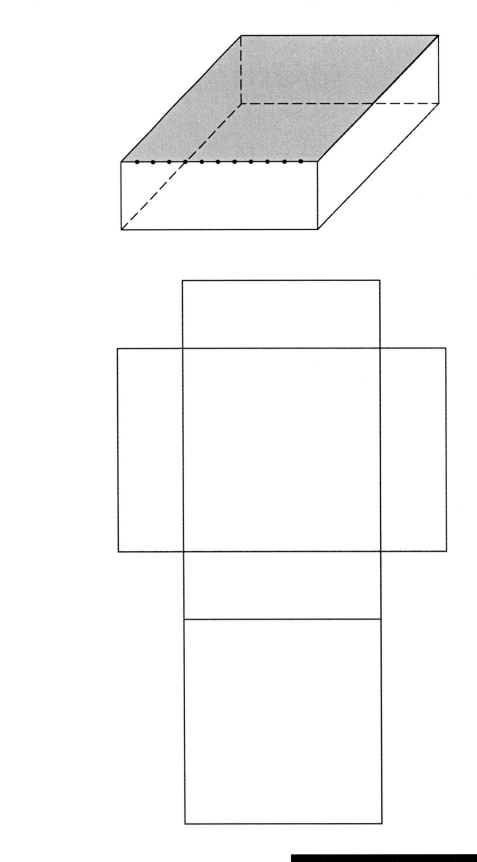

Badger Key Stage 4 Maths Starters

© Badger Publishing Ltd

Year 11 Maths Starter 46 *Shape, space and measures*

Draw nets of simple solids

Objective:
Draw nets of simple solids and use them to evaluate surface area.

Grade: D/C

What you will need:
OHT 45 and 46

Time:
5-10 minutes

Key words:
3D shape, solid, surface area, net, cube, cuboid, prism, face, edge, vertex, vertices

Activity:

Show OHT 45, from the previous starter. Referring to the net on the OHT, ask the students:

Q: Previously we labelled the vertices of this solid. Where on the net of the cuboid would those letter labels go? What do I mean by 'net'?

Invite volunteers to the board to ascribe the letter labels to the vertices on the net. They should also identify the shaded face on the net and the edge marked with 'blobs'.

Q: If we were asked to construct this cuboid out of card, which diagram would help us most in its construction? Would they both be useful? What would the net help us to do? The 3D drawing? If we had dimensions for the cuboid, on which drawing would they be easier to show?

Show OHT 46. Prompt the students to make a sketch of the net of the triangular prism shown.

Give students 3-4 minutes, working in pairs, to solve the problem.

Links to plenary:

Q: How did you do it? Which face did you start with? Why is it easier to begin with the base of the prism? What do I mean by 'prism'? What shape is the sloping face? If we had to make it out of card? Which were the only triangular faces? How could we draw an accurate net? What equipment would we need?

Badger Key Stage 4 Maths Starters

© Badger Publishing Ltd

Year 11: Copymaster for Starter 46 (OHT)

Draw nets of simple solids

Badger Key Stage 4 Maths Starters

© Badger Publishing Ltd

Year 11 Maths Starter 47 *Shape, space and measures*

The circumference of a circle

Objective:
Recall and apply the formulae for the circumference of a circle to solve problems.

Grade: D

What you will need:
OHT 47

Time:
5-10 minutes

Key words:
circle, radius, diameter, circumference, proportion, area, pi, π

Activity:

Show OHT 47. Referring to the first circle, ask the students:

Q: Supposing that the diameter of this circle was roughly 1cm, could you give me an estimate for its circumference? What do I mean by 'circumference'? Is there a relationship between the diameter of a circle and its circumference? Are they in proportion? What do I mean by 'in proportion'? Look at the second circle. The diameter of this circle is four times as big as the first circle. Roughly what will its circumference be? Is it reasonable to say that the circumference is always roughly 3 times the diameter? Can we be more precise? What name do we give to the multiplier that changes diameter into circumference? Is the π symbol used like the letter x symbol? Can π vary? I have a circle with a circumference of roughly 27cm. What is its diameter? How did you work it out? I have a circle which has a circumference of 18m. What is its radius? What did you do?

Prompt students to attempt the exam question on the OHT (D = 1.73m). Give them 2-3 minutes, working in pairs.

Links to plenary:

Q: How did you do it? Was it appropriate to use a calculator? How did you apply the formula for the circumference of a circle? What makes 'real-life' problems like these more challenging than simple 'here's a circle, what's the circumference' type problems? What made it obvious that this was a circle problem? What grade do you think this corresponds to?

Badger Key Stage 4 Maths Starters

© Badger Publishing Ltd

Year 11: Copymaster for Starter 47 (OHT)

The circumference of a circle

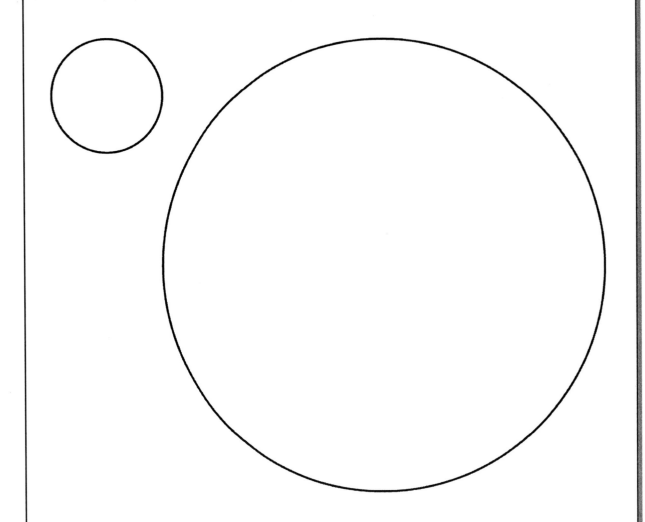

A steel rope, 5.43m long, is wound once around a steel column in a new office block. What is the diameter of the steel column?

Answer: . . . . *(2 marks)*

Badger Key Stage 4 Maths Starters

Year 11 Maths Starter 48 *Shape, space and measures*

The area of a circle

Objective:
Recall and apply the formulae for the area of a circle to solve problems.

Grade: D

What you will need:
OHT 48

Time:
5-10 minutes

Key words:
circle, radius, diameter, circumference, proportion, area, pi, π

Activity:
Ask the students:

Q: How do we calculate the area of a circle? What information about the circle do we need? Suppose we had a circle on a piece of paper - would we have to put a square grid on top and count the squares to get an estimate of the area? Is there a more accurate way? What one measurement would we need to make? Once I know what the radius of the circle is, how do I use that information to calculate the area? How do we remember the formula for the area of a circle? Is there something in the way its sounds - 'pi *are* squared'? What's the value of pi? Can you remember it to 2 decimal places? OK. Let's test our mental calculation skills ~ you can do some jottings to solve this problem but let's not use calculators. A circle has a radius of 4cm. If you use pi = 3.1 or 3.14 if you want to challenge and push your skills, what will the area of the circle be? How did you do it?

Show OHT 48. Prompt students to attempt the exam question (79%). Give them 4-5 minutes, working in pairs.

Links to plenary:

Q: What made this challenging? What things could we work out and write down? What areas can we calculate? Was finding the area of the square reasonably straightforward? The circle? What did you do then? How did you use the two results to calculate the shaded percentage?

Badger Key Stage 4 Maths Starters

© Badger Publishing Ltd

Year 11: Copymaster for Starter 48 (OHT)
The area of a circle

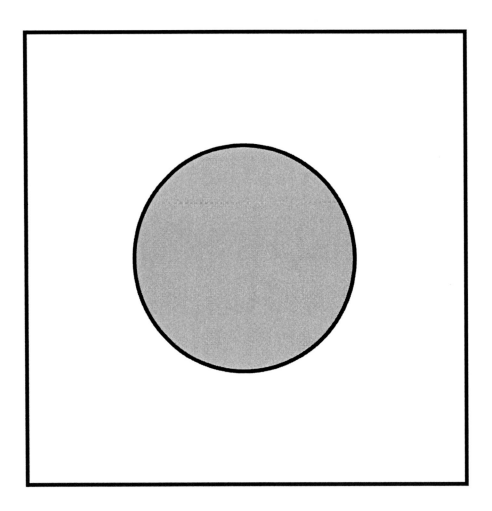

The diagram shows a shaded circle, diameter 4cm, drawn inside a square of side length 8cm. What percentage of the square's area is shaded?

Answer: .... (3 marks)

Badger Key Stage 4 Maths Starters

© Badger Publishing Ltd

Year 11 Maths Starter 49   Shape, space and measures

Convert between units of area or volume

Objective:

Convert between units of area or volume.

Grade: C

What you will need:
OHT 49

Time:
5-10 minutes

Key words:
units of measurement, length, area, volume, congruent

Activity:

Show OHT 49. Ask the students to read the first problem on the OHT.

Q: Is it possible to show that $1m^2$ does not equal $100cm^2$? Who doesn't agree with the statement? Could it be that $1m^2$ is the same as $100cm^2$? Why not? How are we going to show that they aren't equal?

Now prompt students to attempt the problem. Give them 2-3 minutes, working in pairs.

Q: What did you do? Who wrote an explanation down? Can we improve that explanation? Who drew a diagram or pair of diagrams? Why? OK. Let's put together an explanation. (This will involve drawing the figures referred to in the ensuing dialogue on the OHT.) If we start with a square, 1m by 1m, what will its area be? Suppose we drew a congruent square next to it. What do I mean by 'congruent'? This one has its dimensions written on in cm. What is the side length of the square in cm? So what will its area be in cm^2? Have we shown that $1m^2$ does not equal $100cm^2$? Look at the second problem on the OHT. How could we adapt that method to solve this problem?

Give the students 2-3 minutes to discuss this, working in pairs.

Links to plenary:

Q: What did you do? What drawings did you make? How do we convert an area measurement from cm^2 to m^2? A piece of metal has an area of $20\,000cm^2$. What's that in m^2? What did you do? By what did you divide? What about an area of $21\,000cm^2$? $1\,000cm^2$? What simple calculation are we doing every time? How could we convert from m^2 into cm^2?

Badger Key Stage 4 Maths Starters

© Badger Publishing Ltd

Year 11: Copymaster for Starter 49 (OHT)

Convert between units of area or volume

1 Show that 1m² does not equal 100cm².

2 Show that 1 cubic metre does not equal 100 cubic centimetres.

Year 11 Maths Starter 50 — Shape, space and measures

Similar shapes

Objective:
Calculate missing sides of triangles and other shapes (e.g. regular polygons) using similarity.
Grade: B

What you will need:
OHT 50

Time:
10 minutes

Key words:
side lengths, corresponding sides, enlargement, in proportion, similar, multiplier, ratio, triangle, rectangle, polygon, regular

Activity:

Show OHT 50. Ask the students:

Q: What do you notice about triangles 1 and 2? In what way do they make a pair? In what ways is triangle 3 the 'odd one out'? How would you describe the relationship between triangles 1 and 2? Which of the key words would help to describe the relationship? If we think of triangle 2 as an enlargement of triangle 1, what dimensions have changed? Have the angles changed? OK. The height of triangles 1 and 2 are 4cm and 14cm respectively. What problem could I now set? What information would we still need? If the base of triangle 2 is 31.5cm, what's the base of triangle 1?

Give the students 2-3 minutes to attempt the problem, working in pairs.

Q: How did you do it? Where did the number 3.5 come from? Is that the multiplier that changes 4 into 14? Is it useful in this context to call it the scale factor? Can I now assume that the same scale factor will apply between the bases? Will this work for any pair of triangles? Must they be similar triangles? What do I mean by 'similar'?

Prompt students to attempt the exam question on the OHT. Give them 3-4 minutes.

Links to plenary:

Q: How did you do it? What did you do first? How did you use the bases of the two triangles to calculate a scale factor? What did you do next? If the two scale factors are different, what does that tell us? Is it possible that, if we measure the hypotenuses for the two triangles, they would be related by one of the scale factors we have found? Is it possible for two pairs of corresponding sides of a triangle to be in proportion, but not the remaining pair of sides?

Badger Key Stage 4 Maths Starters

© Badger Publishing Ltd

Year 11: Copymaster for Starter 50 (OHT)

Similar shapes

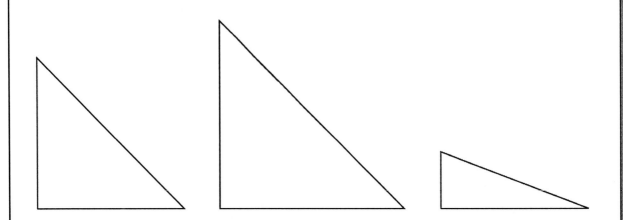

Show that the triangles below are not mathematically similar.

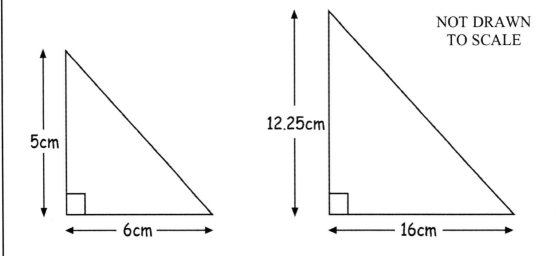

NOT DRAWN TO SCALE

Answer: . . . .   *(2 marks)*

Badger Key Stage 4 Maths Starters

© Badger Publishing Ltd

Year 11 Maths Starter 51 *Shape, space and measures*

Pythagoras' theorem

Objective:
Use Pythagoras' theorem to solve problems in real-life contexts and geometric situations such as bearings, areas of triangles, diagonals of rectangles, etc.

Grade: C

What you will need:
OHT 51

Time:
5-10 minutes

Key words: Pythagoras' theorem, right-angled triangle, hypotenuse, isosceles triangle

Activity:

Explain to the students that you want them to write a simple exam question that might be used to test their understanding of Pythagoras' theorem. Give them 2-3 minutes to devise the question ~ they might work in pairs on this.

Q: Did we all write 'abstract' triangle questions or did anyone put their triangle into a context? If we focus on the abstract problems, how many of you drew diagrams for your question? Is it possible to write a Pythagoras question without a diagram? How? How much information do we need to give in the question? Can you use Pythagoras with only one side? What if the triangle is right-angled and isosceles? How many of us wrote a problem where you gave both of the shorter sides and asked for the hypotenuse? How would you expect a student to solve that kind of problem? What working out would you expect? Who set a problem that would involve subtraction? How? Will the questions always be easily identifiable as Pythagoras problems? What contexts could we use to test Pythagoras? Can you write a problem that tests a knowledge of Pythagoras and the area of a triangle formula? How? How could we devise a volume question that included Pythagoras?

Show OHT 51. Explain that it shows a number of diagrams. Ask the students to discuss how each of these might be used to set a Pythagoras problem. Give them 3-4 minutes to discuss in pairs.

Links to plenary:

Q: How did you use the ship diagram to set a Pythagoras question? What text might go with the problem? Will it include the words 'Pythagoras' theorem'? What about the co-ordinate diagram? What text would go with that problem? What about the square? How would that read as an exam question? Is it useful to think our way into how mathematical skills might be tested by writing problems in this way? Why?

Badger Key Stage 4 Maths Starters

© Badger Publishing Ltd

Year 11: Copymaster for Starter 51 (OHT)
Pythagoras' theorem

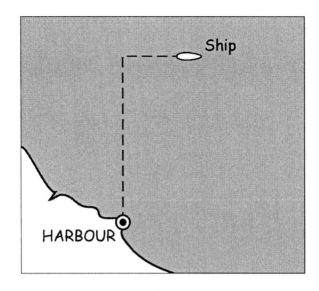

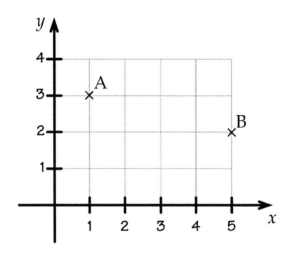

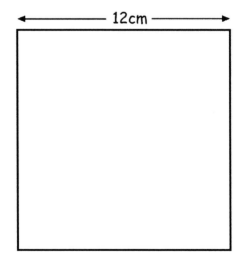

Year 11 Maths Starter 52 — *Shape, space and measures*

Trigonometry 1

Objective:
Use the appropriate ratio to find the lengths of sides in a right-angled triangle.

Grade: B

What you will need:
OHT 52

Time: 5-10 minutes

Key words: right-angled triangle, Pythagoras' theorem, hypotenuse, ratio, opposite, adjacent, angle, sin, cos, tan

Activity:

Show OHT 52. Refer to the text at the top. Ask the students:

Q: How could we complete the second statement? Is there more than one way of completing the statement? Is trigonometry a more flexible skill? What grade does Pythagoras' theorem correspond to? (C) Trigonometry? (B) What makes trig a more challenging skill? How do the words make it appear more challenging? What do the words sin, cos and tan actually mean? How might the word 'ratio' help us to remember what they mean?

Refer to the three triangle diagrams.

Q: If we focus on the given angles and dimensions in each of the three triangles in relation to the given angle, what label would we give to the base of each of these triangles? (adjacent) And the heights of the triangles? (opposite) If we wanted to explore the ratio between these two sides, what ratio are we exploring? (tan) Suppose we work out what the ratio for the 20° triangle is. Would you expect the value of ratio of the 40° triangle to be larger or smaller than that? Why can we see from the triangle that it is going to be larger? What do the two have in common? Which side has increased in length? So, if the opposite is larger and the adjacent remains the same, does that justify our prediction? How many times larger will it be? How many times larger will tan 60° be? Why? Is tan 80° much larger? Why? What's tan 89°? What's happening? What's tan 90°? Why is there no such value?

Links to plenary:

Q: What's the ratio of the adjacent to the hypotenuse for the 20° triangle? What ratio are we exploring now? (cos) Which is derived by dividing what by what? If we work out the cos ratio for the 40° triangle, will it be smaller or larger than that for the 20° triangle? What is cos 40°? Why is it smaller? If the adjacent has stayed the same and the hypotenuse has increased?

Badger Key Stage 4 Maths Starters

© Badger Publishing Ltd

Trigonometry 1

Year 11: Copymaster for Starter 52 (OHT)

For right angled triangles:

Pythagoras' theorem is used to find a *missing side* when you know the *two other sides*.

Trigonometry is used to find .... when you know ....

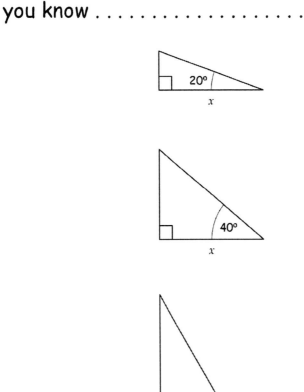
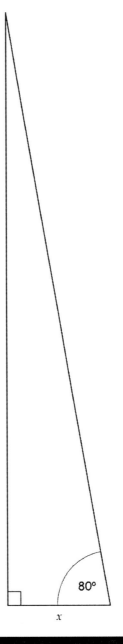

Badger Key Stage 4 Maths Starters

Year 11 Maths Starter 53 — Shape, space and measures

Trigonometry 2

Objective:
Find angles of elevation and depression using the appropriate ratio.
Grade: B

What you will need:
OHT 53

Time:
5-10 minutes

Key words:
right-angled triangle, Pythagoras' theorem, hypotenuse, ratio, opposite, adjacent, angle, sin, cos, tan

Activity:

Ask the students to devise a simple problem that might be used to test a basic understanding of trigonometry. Give them 2-3 minutes to devise their problems.

Q: Did we all devise abstract problems? If we focus on those, did everyone sketch a diagram? Is it possible to set a trig question without a diagram? Why is it harder to set one without a diagram? Who set a problem where you gave a side and an angle and were looking for another side? What other type of problem could we set? How? How would you expect a student to solve your problem? What working out would you expect?

Ask the students to devise a second trig problem, this time in context. Give them 2-3 minutes to devise their problems. You might suggest some possible contexts if they struggle.

Q: What contexts can we use? Did anyone set a problem involving a ship travelling away from harbour? What information would we need to supply? What text would go with that question? Would we include the word 'trigonometry'? What other types of problems did you write? How?

Links to plenary:

Show OHT 53.

Q: How could we use these diagrams to set a problem? If the figure in each diagram could measure the angles shown using a special piece of equipment? What could we use those angles to find? What would those angles be called? Which dimensions would be easy to measure or control in each situation? Is this how the heights of tall buildings or trees can be measured?

Badger Key Stage 4 Maths Starters

© Badger Publishing Ltd

Year 11: Copymaster for Starter 53 (OHT)
Trigonometry 2

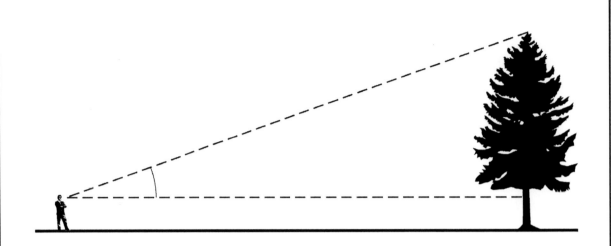

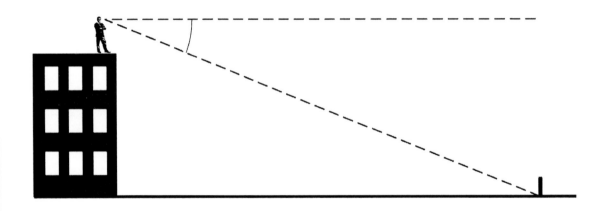

Badger Key Stage 4 Maths Starters

© Badger Publishing Ltd

Year 11 Maths Starter 54   *Shape, space and measures*

Trigonometry and Pythagoras problems

Objective:
Apply trigonometric ratios and Pythagoras' theorem to solve assorted problems, including those involving bearings.

Grade: B

What you will need:
OHT 54

Time:
5-10 minutes

Key words:
right-angled triangle, Pythagoras' theorem, hypotenuse, ratio, opposite, adjacent, angle, sin, cos, tan, bearings

Activity:

Show OHT 54. Ask the students:

Q: What's missing from this exam question? What might you expect to accompany it? Can we sketch a diagram from the information given? How? Where are we going to site the coastguard? What next? Do we use dotted lines to show the distance north and east that the ship has travelled in? Where on the sketch can we show the two unknowns that we are being asked to find? How are we going to solve the first problem?

Give students 1-2 minutes to discuss this in pairs.

Q: How are we going to find the distance from coastguard to boat? Why might this be described as a classic Pythagoras problem? Did you immediately recognise it as a Pythagoras problem when you read it? Did it help to draw the sketch? How did you use the theorem to solve the problem? How are we going to work out the bearing on which the rescue boat should sail?

Give students 2-3 minutes to discuss this in pairs.

Links to plenary:

Q: How are we going to do it? Which ratio are we going to use? In the context of the question, which distance is 'opposite' the angle that we want? Adjacent to it? What's the hypotenuse in the context of this question? How did you use trig to calculate the angle? To what degree of accuracy should we give the angle? Remember - lives are at stake. Do we give the bearing as a two digit number with a number of decimal places? What conventions relate to the giving of bearings?

Badger Key Stage 4 Maths Starters

© Badger Publishing Ltd

Year 11: Copymaster for Starter 54 (OHT)

Trigonometry and Pythagoras problems

A ship has sailed north from the coastguard for 46km, then sailed due east for 27km. It is now stationary and in distress. A ship is to launch from the coastguard.

Calculate:

1 The shortest distance from coastguard to the ship.

   Answer:............................ *(2 marks)*

2 The bearing on which the rescue ship must sail.

   Answer:............................ *(3 marks)*

Badger Key Stage 4 Maths Starters

Year 11 Maths Starter 55 *Shape, space and measures*

Trig in three dimensions

Objective:
Solve problems involving trigonometry in three dimensions.

Grade: B

What you will need:
OHT 55

Time:
5-10 minutes

Key words:
right-angled triangle, Pythagoras' theorem, hypotenuse, ratio, opposite, adjacent, angle, sin, cos, tan, bearings, cuboid

Activity:

Show OHT 55. Ask the students:

Q: What is the name of this solid? How have letter symbols been used to label them? What name would we give the base of the cuboid? (EFGH) What name would we give to the diagonal which has been drawn inside the cuboid? (HC) How could we work out the length of that diagonal?

Give students 3-4 minutes to discuss this in pairs.

Q: Why might it help to draw a line across the base of the cuboid joining H and F? Is that the base of a right-angled triangle with HC as its hypotenuse? How does that help? What's the height of that triangle? Would it help to make a separate sketch of the triangle in 2D? How could we find the length of HF? Is that the hypotenuse of another right-angled triangle on the bottom face of the cuboid? What maths are we going to use to calculate the missing lengths?

Give students 2-3 minutes to work out the lengths HF and HC in pairs. (20.6cm and 21.75cm)

Links to plenary:

Q: How could we work out the size of the angle between HC and the base of the cuboid? Do we know all the sides of the right-angled triangle HCF? What trig ratio could we use? What is the size of the angle? (18.8°) How did you find it? What makes using Pythagoras and trig in 3D so challenging? How does it help to make separate 2D sketches?

Badger Key Stage 4 Maths Starters

© Badger Publishing Ltd

Trig in three dimensions

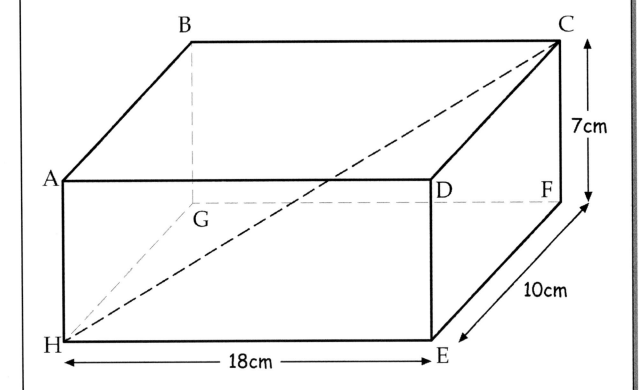

Year 11 Maths Starter 56	Shape, space and measures

Loci constructions 1

Objective:
Construct perpendicular bisectors using only compasses and a ruler.
Grade: C

What you will need:
OHT 56
Time:
5-10 minutes

Key words: rhombus, parallel, arc, bisector, perpendicular, angle bisector, equidistant, diagonal, line of symmetry

Activity:

Ask the students:

Q: What are the properties of the rhombus? What do I mean by 'properties'? If I sketch a rhombus on the board, how would I show that all the sides are equal? Are any of the angles equal? How many lines of symmetry does it have? Are these the diagonals of the shape? What do you notice about the diagonals?

Draw a straight horizontal line on the board, about 50cm. Ask students to draw a similar line in their books, about 10cm.

Q: How might we use compasses and a ruler to construct an isosceles triangle with this line as its base? How could we extend that to turn our drawing of an isosceles triangle into a drawing of a rhombus? Would it be much more challenging? Do we need to change the settings on our compass?

Give students 1-2 minutes to complete their rhombus constructions.

Q: How could we use the construction to test the properties of a rhombus? Why do I call it a 'construction' and not a drawing? If we join the two unconnected vertices with a dotted line, what have I done to the straight line that we started with? Have I cut it into two? Into what fractions have I cut the line? Why *must* we have bisected the line? Can you use the properties of a rhombus to explain? At what angle have we bisected the line? Can you justify that statement? How might this skill be useful?

Links to plenary:

Q: Would it help if I joined the two points together? Show OHT 56. Where on the OHT will the region containing all the points closer to A than B be? Closer to B than A? When will one region become the other? Why will it be useful to find the line that shows all the points equidistant from A and B? What do I mean by 'equidistant'? How will today's skill help us?

Badger Key Stage 4 Maths Starters

© Badger Publishing Ltd

Year 11: Copymaster for Starter 56 (OHT)

Loci constructions 1

Shade the region including all points closer to A than B on this diagram:

x B

A x

(2 marks)

Badger Key Stage 4 Maths Starters

© Badger Publishing Ltd

Year 11 Maths Starter 57 — Shape, space and measures

Loci constructions 2

Objective:
Construct angle bisectors using only compasses and a ruler.

Grade: C

What you will need: OHT 57

Time: 5-10 minutes

Key words:
rhombus, parallel, arc, bisector, perpendicular, angle bisector, equidistant, diagonal, line of symmetry

Activity:

Ask the students:

Q: Can you remember the properties of the rhombus? What was special about the diagonals of the rhombus? How do they cut each other? What do they do to the angles of the rhombus? Draw a point on the board. Ask students to conceive of the points as the uppermost vertex of an isosceles triangle.

Q: How could we use this to construct an isosceles triangle where the equal sides were, for example, 5cm? Give the students 2-3 minutes to construct the two equal sides but warn them not to draw in the third side.

Q: What have we drawn so far? What would a Year 7 student call the diagram? (an angle) How could we extend what we've done to turn our drawing of an angle into a drawing of a rhombus? What would we be looking for? (The fourth vertex.) How would we find it? Give the students 1-2 minutes to find the fourth vertex but warn them not to draw in any new sides.

Q: If we join this point to the opposite vertex, the point we began with, what have we done to the angle we drew? How might the ability to bisect an angle be useful? Show OHT 57. Explain that this is an exam question which could be used to test the skill they have just practiced. Ask the students to consider how.

Links to plenary:

Q: Where on the OHT will the region containing all the points closer to line P than line Q be? Closer to Q than P? When will one region become the other? Why will it be useful to find the line that shows all the points equidistant from P and Q? What do I mean by 'equidistant'? How will today's skill help us?

Badger Key Stage 4 Maths Starters

© Badger Publishing Ltd

Loci constructions 2

Shade the region including all points closer to the line P than the line Q on this diagram:

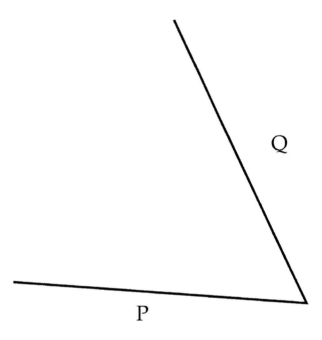

(2 marks)

Year 11 Maths Starter 58 *Shape, space and measures*

Circle theorems

Objective:
Understand and use circle theorems.

Grade: B

What you will need:
OHT 58, class set of worksheets, class set of protractors.

Time:
5-10 minutes

Key words:
circle, circumference, radius, diameter, tangent, angle, arc, chord, segment, subtend

Activity:

Show OHT 58 and distribute class set. Prompt the students to draw a radius on the circle. Now model drawing a line which just touches the circle at the point where the radius meets the circumference. Explain that this line is known as a tangent to the circle.

Q: What do you notice about the tangent and the radius we've drawn? At what angle does it appear that they meet? How could we test this observation? Is it possible to draw a tangent and radius that won't be perpendicular? OK. We've established one of the circle theorem: a tangent to a circle is perpendicular to the radius. We're going to try another.

Draw a chord in the circle on the OHT. Explain that you have divided the circle into two segments. Join the ends of the chord to any point on the circumference. Now join the ends to another point on the circumference. Ask students to do this with their circles.

Q: What do you notice about the two angles you've drawn? How could we test that observation? Is it possible to draw an angle in this segment that isn't equal to these two? How could we put our new theorem into words?

Finally, draw two points on the circumference and join them to an opposite point on the circumference and the centre of the circle. Prompt students to do likewise.

Links to plenary:

Q: What do you notice? How could we test that observation? Will it work for any pair of angles drawn in this way? What if I increase the distance between the two points that I drew on the circumference to begin with? What happens if they become further apart? How could we put our new theorem into words?

Badger Key Stage 4 Maths Starters

© Badger Publishing Ltd

Year 11: Copymaster for Starter 58 (OHT)
Circle theorems

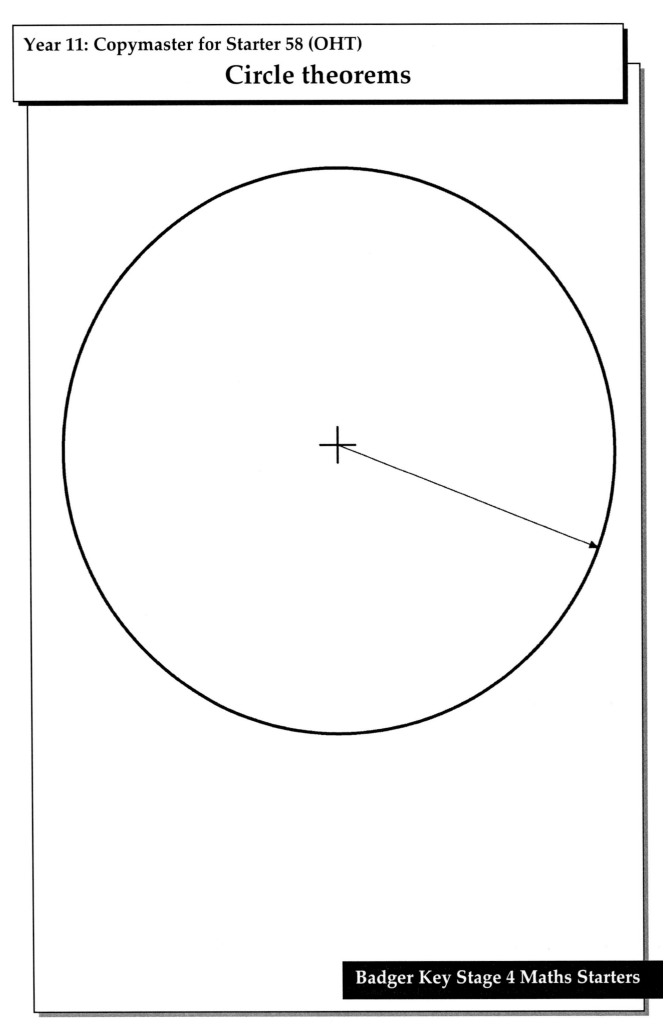

Badger Key Stage 4 Maths Starters

© Badger Publishing Ltd

Year 11 Maths Starter 59	Shape, space and measures

Length, area or volume formulae

Objective:
Recognise whether a formula represents a length, area or volume by considering its dimensions.

Grade: B

What you will need:
OHT 59

Time:
5-10 minutes

Key words:
2D shape, congruent, axis, axes, vertical, horizontal, transform, translate, vertex, vertices

Activity:

Explain to the students:

Imagine I have a box of straight metal wires that come in three lengths, a, b and c. I'm going to combine them to make lengths, 2D shapes and 3D solids ~ but I'm not going to tell you whether I've made a length or a plane shape or a solid. I want you to decide what dimension I'm working in by looking at a formula for the combination of wires I've made.

Show OHT 59. Refer to the first three formulae one by one.

Q: What's the first formula referring to? If we add a length of wire to a length of wire? So adding two lengths makes another length. What about ab? What formula involves multiplying lengths? What kind of shape am I finding the area for? So multiply two lengths together and we create a 2D shape that has area. What about $2c$?

Give students 2-3 minutes to identify whether the remaining formulae represent length, area or volume. They should work in pairs.

Links to plenary:

Q: How did you do it? What did c^2 represent? Is that a length multiplied by a length? What about $bc + a$? Could that be a volume formula? Why not? What would turn it into a volume formula? What about abc?

Badger Key Stage 4 Maths Starters

© Badger Publishing Ltd

Year 11: Copymaster for Starter 59 (OHT)

Length, area or volume formulae

$a + b$

ab

$2c$

c^2

$bc + a$

abc

Badger Key Stage 4 Maths Starters

Year 11 Maths Starter 60 — *Shape, space and measures*

Length, area and volume scale factors

Objective:

Understand the effect an enlargement has on the area and volume of a shape, by considering scale factors; i.e. that where the length scale factor is x, the area has been multiplied by x^2.

Grade: D/C

What you will need:
OHT 60

Time:
5-10 minutes

Key words:
2D shape, congruent, similar, enlargement, scale factor, side length, area, volume

Activity:

Show OHT 60. Ask the students:

Q: How would you describe these two shapes? What word would you use to describe the relationship between these two triangles? Are they congruent triangles? What do I mean by 'congruent'? Are they similar? What does that tell us about the two shapes? What things about the two shapes have changed? What has stayed the same? What scale factor has been used to enlarge triangle 1 to create its image, triangle 2?

Give students 1-2 minutes to calculate the scale factor.

Q: How did you work it out? OK. Listen to this statement: 'The scale factor was 2.7. So the area of triangle 2 will be 2.7 times the area of triangle 1.' True or false?

Give students 2-3 minutes to discuss this in pairs.

Links to plenary:

Q: How could we test the statement? Did anyone begin to work out the areas? What's the area of triangle 1? 2? Did anyone find the scale factor? What did you notice? Is there any link between the area scale factor, 7.29, and the length scale factor, 2.7? Can we explain why applying the area scale factor is like applying the length scale factor twice? What would happen if we used a scale factor on a cuboid that had a volume? How could we test that theory?

Badger Key Stage 4 Maths Starters

© Badger Publishing Ltd

Year 11: Copymaster for Starter 60 (OHT)
Length, area or volume scale factors

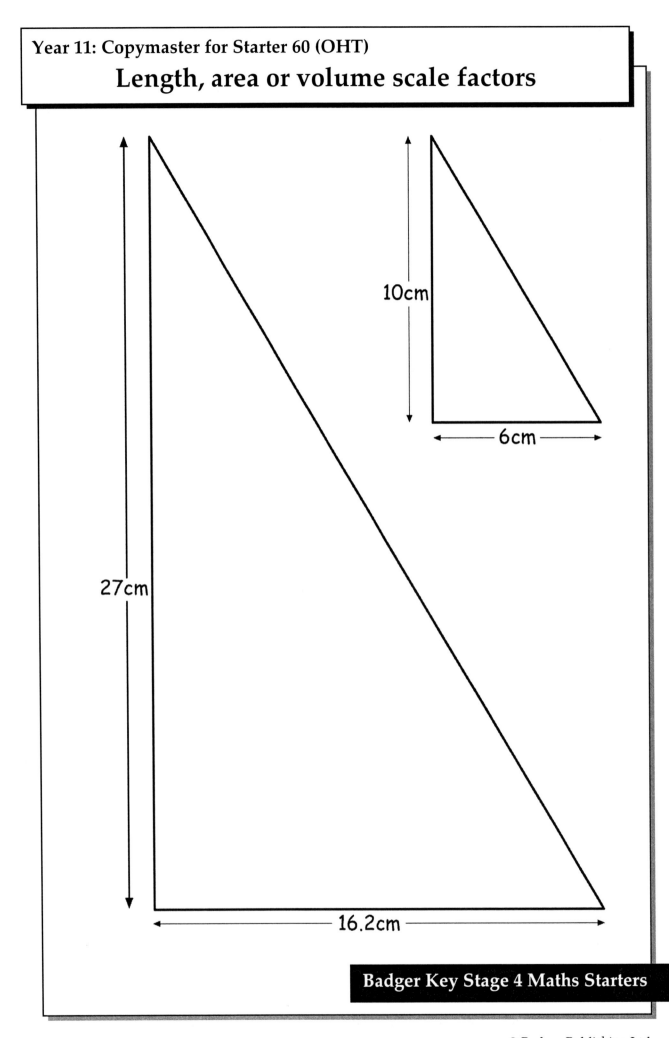

Year 11 Maths Starter 61 — Handling Data

Suggest a complex hypothesis

Objective:

Suggest a hypothesis and consider the statistical methods needed to investigate it.

Grade: D/C/B/A

What you will need:
OHT 61

Time:
5-10 minutes

Key words:
data, hypothesis, test, predict, collect

Activity:

Show OHT 61. Explain to the students that it shows a number of hypotheses and several statistical diagrams.

Q: What do I mean by 'hypothesis'? How is it useful to form a hypothesis first when conducting a data-handling investigation? What are the names of the diagrams shown?

Prompt the students to match each hypothesis with **one** of the diagrams shown on the OHT. Give them 4-5 minutes to discuss the problem in pairs.

Q: How did you do it? Which diagram might be used to prove the first hypothesis? How does the scatter compare two sets of related data? What name might we give to the vertical axis? Horizontal? Do you think the hypothesis is true? Can we use the scatter diagram to make predictions? How? Which diagram might be used to prove the second hypothesis? Could it be either the bar-chart or the pie-chart? Why might the pie-chart be better? What does 'majority' mean? From which diagram would it be easier to see that one group is in the majority? Is it possible that rap might be the most popular but not be in the majority?

Links to plenary:

Q: How is the box-and-whisker diagram used to show the validity of a hypothesis like the fourth? Which diagram represents the boys? How can you tell? Is the hypothesis true? Why is it useful to compare the spread for the middle 50%?

Badger Key Stage 4 Maths Starters

© Badger Publishing Ltd

Year 11: Copymaster for Starter 61 (OHT)
Suggest a complex hypothesis

'The higher the number of hits on the website, the more CDs sold that day.'

'The majority of people think the war was a mistake.'

'The most popular type of music amongst Year 11 students is rap.'

'Although the spread of marks will be wider for boys, the spread of marks for the middle 50% of the boys will be similar to the spread for the middle 50% of girls.'

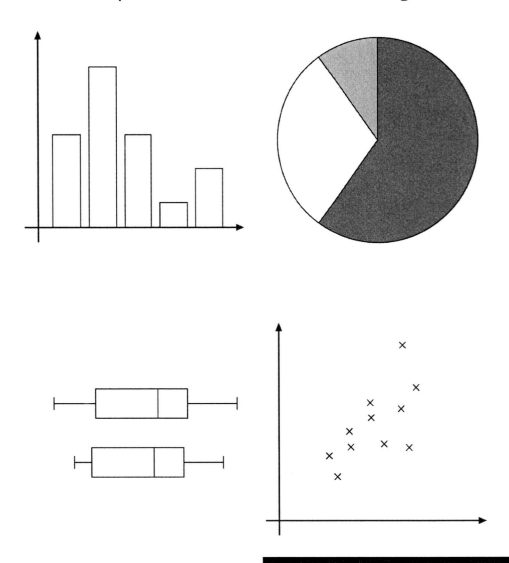

Badger Key Stage 4 Maths Starters

Year 11 Maths Starter 62

Handling Data

Plan an enquiry

Objective:
Begin to plan an enquiry relating to a chosen hypothesis.

Grade: C

What you will need:
OHT 61

Time:
5-10 minutes

Key words:
data, hypothesis, test, predict, collect, questionnaire, survey, bias

Activity:

Show OHT 61 from the previous starter. Ask the students:

Q: If we wanted to investigate the first hypothesis, what data would we need? Suppose you run a website that sells CDs. What data would you want to collect? Can a website record the number of 'hits' per day? And keep a record of the number of CDs sold? How many days should we record this data for? Is a week enough? How about three years' worth of data? Should we expect the correlation between hits and sales to stay the same all year round? Are there any times of the year when everybody buys lots of things like CDs and DVDs? Should we ignore December completely? Will there still be a link between hits and sales?

How would we collect data for the second hypothesis? What do we mean by 'people'? Is the following a good question for our survey: 'Do you agree that the war was a terrible mistake?' Will the data for the third hypothesis be easier to collect? Why?

Links to plenary:

Q: What data would we collect for the fourth hypothesis? Suppose we're interested in comparing girls' and boys' performance in the KS3 maths exam. How many test scores could we collect? Should we just collect their overall levels or obtain their actual exam scores? How do the box-and-whisker diagrams help us to compare boys' and girls' scores? Are they, on average, quite similar? What about the spread of the scores?

Badger Key Stage 4 Maths Starters

© Badger Publishing Ltd

Year 11 Maths Starter 63 Handling Data

Take a sample

Objective:
Select and justify a method of sampling; appreciate that a larger sample size will give a more accurate estimate.

Grade: D/C

What you will need:
OHTs 61 and 63.

Time:
5-10 minutes

Key words:
data, hypothesis, test, predict, collect

Activity:
Show OHT 61 from the previous starter. Ask the students:

Q: Imagine we are investigating the third hypothesis and we have information on the musical preferences of 421 Year 11 students, from a number of different schools. Are we going to try and process all of that data? What do I mean by 'process'? What sort of things can we do with data? Will we use it all? How much data do we need? Should we just take the first 100 students and throw out the data for the other 321? What if all of those 100 students are from a grammar school? Will that school accurately represent the whole borough? So what sampling method should we use? What do I mean by 'sampling method'? What different types of sampling method do we know?

Show OHT 63. Explain that it shows four types of data sets from which we might take a sample. Prompt them to decide, for each of the sets, how many items to include in the sample and what sampling technique to employ. Give them 5-7 minutes to discuss this in pairs.

Links to plenary:
Q: How many eggs should we test to see if any of them are rotten? What kind of sampling technique? Should we only sample eggs from the upper rows in the container? Will a simple random sample be appropriate? Or a systematic sample? How might we do that? How could we take a sample of forty students from the second data set? Can we just pick the first forty? Why not? Are we more likely to get an even sample from the third data set by picking the first 40? Why? What about the fourth data set? Should we pick 30 Year 7s and 30 Year 11s? Why not? What should we do?

Badger Key Stage 4 Maths Starters

© Badger Publishing Ltd

Year 11: Copymaster for Starter 63 (OHT)

Take a sample

120 eggs packed in boxes, stacked in a container.

The names of 200 students in age order.

The names of 200 students listed alphabetically.

The names of 80 Year 7 students and 56 Year 11 students, listed alphabetically.

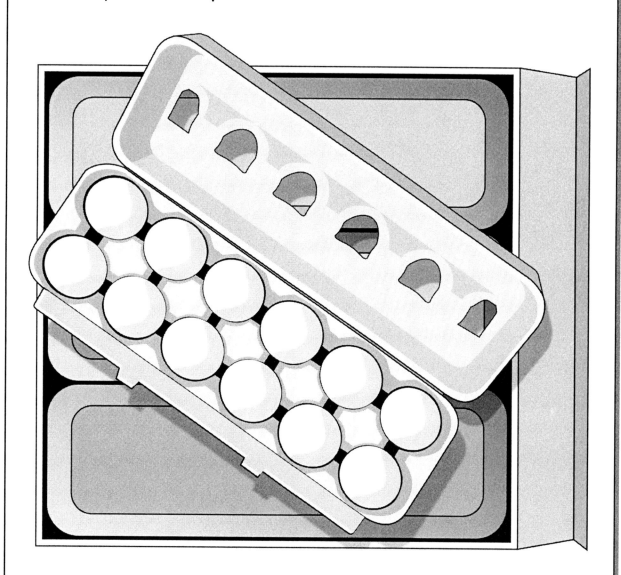

Badger Key Stage 4 Maths Starters

© Badger Publishing Ltd

Year 11 Maths Starter 64	Handling Data

Two-way tables

Objective:
Design and use two-way tables for discrete and continuous data.

Grade: E/D

What you will need:
OHT 64

Time:
5 minutes

Key words:
data, hypothesis, test, table, two-way table, frequency

Activity:

Show OHT 64. Ask the students:

Q: What does the table show? How is it representing the information? Is it telling us more than one thing about the students in the table? How is it doing this? Why might such tables be called 'two-way tables'? Can we identify how many students there are in each tutor group? Can we identify how many students have yet to complete their coursework in Year 11? Can we identify the total number of Year 11 students in the cohort? How could we complete the table?

Give students 1-2 minutes to find the missing values for the table. They should work independently on this task.

Links to plenary:

Q: How did you do it? Roughly what fraction of the Year group has completed coursework? How can we calculate a more accurate figure? Does the table give us all the information we need? What other tables or diagrams allow us to show two different types of information? Could we use this table to draw a dual bar-chart? How?

Badger Key Stage 4 Maths Starters

Year 11: Copymaster for Starter 64 (OHT)

Two-way tables

Coursework completion table

	11FC	11JC	11BF	Total
Completed	14	22		
Not completed	15		8	
Total		31	27	

Year 11 Maths Starter 65 — Handling Data

Compare correlations

Objective:

Use two scatter graphs to compare correlations.

Grade: C/B

What you will need:
OHT 65

Time:
5-10 minutes

Key words:

data, hypothesis, test, scatter diagram, correlation, weak correlation, strong correlation, positive correlation, negative correlation

Activity:

Show OHT 65. Ask the students:

Q: What's shown here? What's similar about the correlations shown? Do they both show negative correlations? What's different about them? OK. I'm going to read you some types of correlation and I want you to decide which scatter represents each one. 'The height of some students and their shoe size.' Will that be a positive correlation? Is it likely to be a very strong correlation? What would correlate more strongly with height? Why might inside leg measurement correlate better with height? Let's try another: 'The cost of a book and the number of pages.' Will there be a correlation? Strong or weak? What factors might spoil the correlation? Will there be a correlation between students' IQ and their KS3 average? What do I mean by 'KS3 average'?

Suppose we decided to investigate the correlation between KS3 scores and IQ in more depth. We draw one scatter for IQ against English score and one scatter for IQ against Maths score. Which will be English and which will be maths?

Give students 1 minute to discuss the problem in pairs.

Links to plenary:

Q: Which was which? Can you justify your answer? Why might maths more closely correlate with IQ? Suppose we decided to investigate IQ and its impact on exam performance from another angle. We draw one scatter for IQ against KS3 average score for girls, one for IQ against KS3 average score for boys. Which is which? Why might there be a closer correlation for girls? What spoils the correlation for boys? Does this mean that girls are more intelligent? Or are the boys underachieving? What do I mean by 'underachieving'?

Badger Key Stage 4 Maths Starters

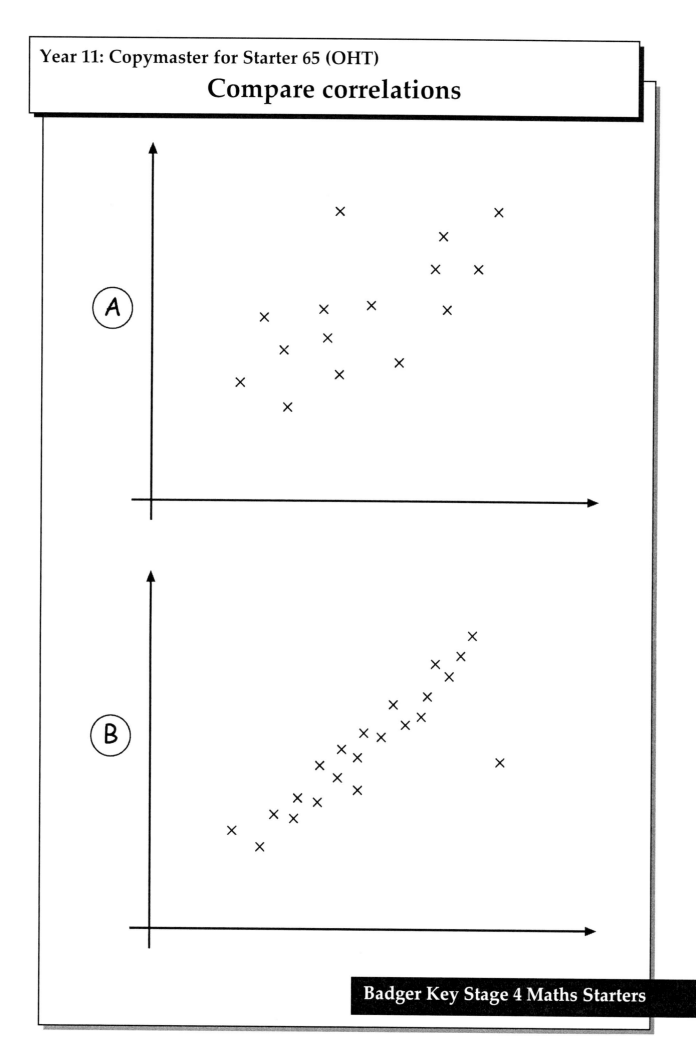

Year 11 Maths Starter 66   **Handling Data**

Estimates for the mean and median

Objective:
Calculate estimates for the mean and median for grouped continuous data.

Grade: C

What you will need:
OHT 66

Time: 5-10 minutes

Key words:
data, hypothesis, test, average, represent, central tendency, mean, median, mode, continuous

Activity:

Show OHT 66. Ask the students:

Q: What's shown here? What kind of table is it? What data does it show? Does it show the data as individual pieces of data? How many students weighed exactly 73kg? Why can we not say? What have they done to the data? Why do we group data? How does it help us to spot patterns and trends? Can we just spot patterns by knowing the number of students who weigh 71kg, and then the number who weigh 72kg, 73kg and so on? How might all that detail hide any trends? If we had the weights of ten students, how would we work out the *average* weight?

Can we work out the average weight for the students shown in the table? Why not? Can we work out an estimate? How? If we look at the 6 students in the first weight group, what values could their weights be? Can we make a guess? Should we assume that they all weigh 41kg? Would that be an underestimate? 49kg? Can we assume that they would all average out to about 45kg? If we have those six students who we assume weigh 45kg each, what would their total weight be? What should we do next? Will we end up with an estimate for the total weight of all 40 students? How? What then?

Links to plenary:

Q: How could we work out an estimate for the median for this data? Out of 40 students, which student would be the middle student? Can we round that to student 20 for the sake of making our estimate easier? Into which group will student 20 fall? How can we work that out? What number student is the first to fall into this group? The last? Is student 20 half way between them? If they were, would that make estimating their weight easier? How? How can we adapt that method since student 20 is not halfway along the group?

Badger Key Stage 4 Maths Starters

© Badger Publishing Ltd

Year 11: Copymaster for Starter 66 (OHT)
Estimates for the mean and median

Weight	Frequency		
40 - 49kg	6		
50 - 59kg	16		
60 - 69kg	10		
70 - 79kg	8		

Year 11 Maths Starter 67 — Handling Data

Compare two distributions

Objective:
Compare distributions using measures of range and spread.

Grade: D/C

What you will need:
OHT 67

Time: 5-10 minutes

Key words:
data, hypothesis, average, represent, central tendency, mean, median, mode, spread, range

Activity:

Show OHT 67. Ask the students:

Q: The tables show the hand-spans of two groups of people. What do I mean by 'hand-span'? Can you estimate what your hand-span is? How could we measure it more accurately? With what other data could we expect hand-span to correlate? How could we compare the two groups of people? Which group is composed only of Year 11s or adults? How can we tell? How much greater is the average hand-span of group B when compared to group A? How could we decide? Which group has a mode? Does that help us in this situation? How could we work out the median? How can we work out the mean?

Give students 3-4 minutes to find the averages, working in pairs.

Links to plenary:

Q: Why are the averages used to represent a group when comparing it to another? Would it be fair to use the largest value for both? Or the smallest? Why do we use a value which describes the 'central tendency' of a group? What do you think I mean by 'central tendency'?

Which group has both adults and younger students? What statistic could we use to confirm this?

Badger Key Stage 4 Maths Starters

© Badger Publishing Ltd

Year 11: Copymaster for Starter 67 (OHT)

Compare two distributions

Group A	Group B
14cm	16cm
20cm	25cm
11cm	17cm
15cm	22cm
10cm	19cm
22cm	19cm
24cm	

Year 11 Maths Starter 68

Handling Data

Use cumulative frequency curves

Objective:
Solve problems using a cumulative frequency curve (e.g. *How many ____ were more than...*); use cumulative frequency curves to estimate the median, lower quartile, upper quartile and interquartile ranges.

Grade: B

What you will need:
OHT 68

Time:
5-10 minutes

Key words:
data, hypothesis, frequency, average, represent, central tendency, mean, median, mode, spread, range, cumulative frequency, upper quartile, lower quartile, interquartile range

Activity:
Show OHT 68. Ask the students:

Q: What data is shown in the table? How has the data been shown - as values or as grouped frequencies? What do I mean by 'grouped frequencies'? What is the modal group? Could we use the table to get an estimate for the mean height? How? How many students measured were less than 150cm tall? How can we use the table to work that out? How many students were taller than 1.6m? Why do you think there are less people in the 'lower than 140cm' and 'higher than 179cm' groups? If we wanted to work out a measure of the spread of the data, how could we do that?

Model finding the cumulative frequencies and plot them on the axes. Where groups have met the idea of cumulative frequency before, they should be required to tell you how to do this.

Links to plenary:

Q: How could we use the curve to get an estimate for the median height? If we asked all 68 students to stand in height order and then separated them into two groups, which number student would be the tallest in the first group? Or the shortest in the second group? What might an estimate of the height of student 34 be? How could we work out the range? Why might the spread between the middle 50% of the group be a better measure of spread? Do the very short and very tall students make the spread appear wider than it is? Are most of these students quite similar in height?

Badger Key Stage 4 Maths Starters

© Badger Publishing Ltd

Use cumulative frequency curves

Year 9 students

Height (cm)	Frequency	
130 - 139	5	
140 - 149	15	
150 - 159	25	
160 - 169	12	
170 - 179	6	

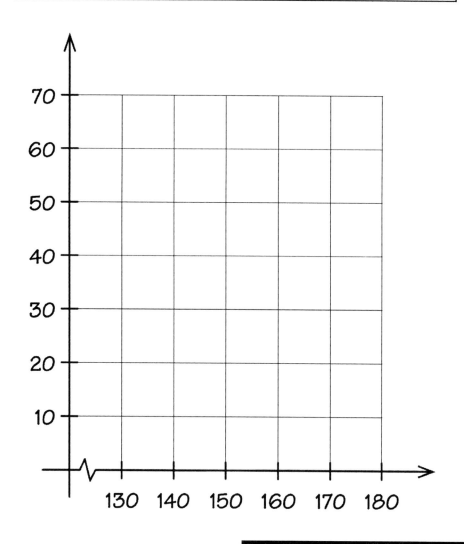

Year 11 Maths Starter 69 — Handling Data

Compare two box-plot diagrams

Objective:

Compare two box-plots.

Grade: C

What you will need:
OHT 69

Time:
5-10 minutes

Key words:

data, hypothesis, test, frequency, average, represent, central tendency, mean, median, mode, spread, range, cumulative frequency, upper quartile, lower quartile, interquartile range, box-plots, box-and-whisker diagrams

Activity:

Show OHT 69. Refer to the first box-and-whisker. Ask the students:

Q: How has this been drawn? How has the cumulative frequency curve for the boys been used to draw this 'box-plot'? What's the median height for the boys? How is this shown on the box-plot? How are the upper and lower quartiles shown? Why do you think these diagrams are sometimes called 'box-and-whisker' diagrams? What do you think the 'whiskers' show? So, does this diagram show us something that the cumulative frequency curve can't show us? What other advantages over the cumulative frequency curve does the box-plot have? How can we use it to compare two distributions? What comparisons can we make between the heights of these two groups of students, based on the box-plots?

Give students 2-3 minutes to discuss the two distributions in pairs.

Links to plenary:

Q: What interpretations did you make? What do I mean by 'interpretation'? On average, who was taller, boys or girls? How can we use the box-plot to show this? Is 'the median was larger for the girls than the boys' an interpretation or just a description of where the medians are? What's the difference? Should an interpretation say something about the differences in growth patterns between boys and girls? Are the heights of the middle 50% of the boys evenly spread about the median? True or false: 'There are more boys between the lower quartile and the median than between the median and the upper quartile.'

Badger Key Stage 4 Maths Starters

Year 11: Copymaster for Starter 69 (OHT)
Compare two box-plot diagrams

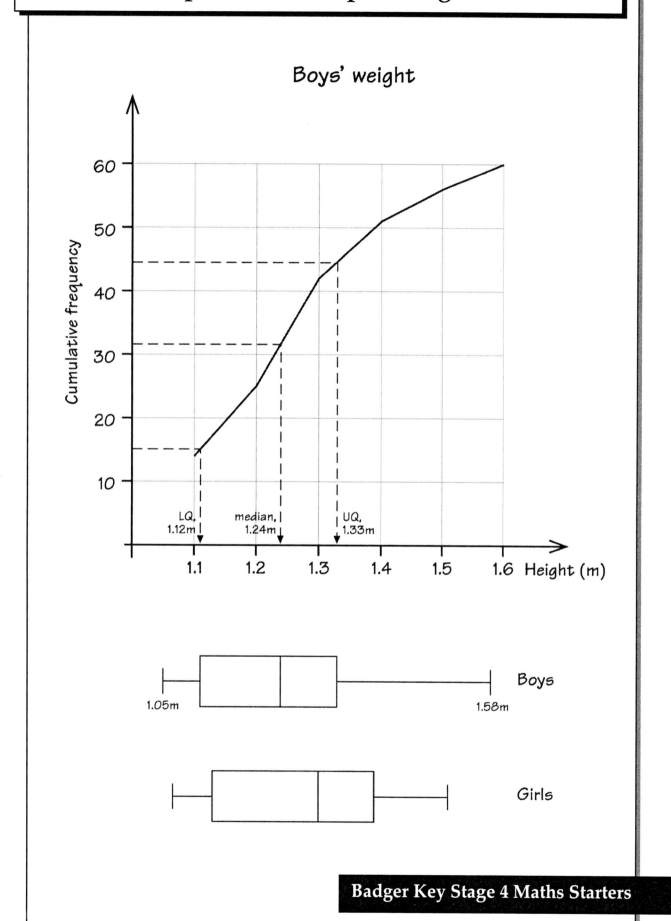

Badger Key Stage 4 Maths Starters

Year 11 Maths Starter 70   Handling Data

Time series

Objective:
Draw and produce line graphs for time series.

Grade: C

What you will need:
OHT 70, class set of worksheets.

Time: 5-10 minutes

Key words:
data, hypothesis, plot, time series, line graph, trend line

Activity:
Show OHT 70. Referring to the table, ask the students:

Q: What is this table showing us? Is it several sets of data? Is it one piece of data that's been recorded over a period of time? Have they recorded the data for a number of years? How many times per year did they record the data? Why do you think they did that? What's a 'quarter'? Do you notice any annual patterns? Are there quarters when sales are traditionally higher? Why do you think that might be? Are there any other patterns? Why is it difficult to spot clear patterns from the numbers alone? Did sales improve over the four years recorded here? Would a line graph help us to identify trends and patterns? How could we use the set of axes to draw a line graph?

Distribute class set of worksheets. Give students 3-4 minutes to plot a line graph, joining the points with straight dashed lines.

Links to plenary:

Q: How did you do it? Does the graph make annual patterns easier to identify? In which quarters do sales drop? Why might that be? Why might these values be referred to as a 'time series'? Is the trend of sales upwards? How could we draw a trend line to show that they are?

Is it a little like drawing a line of best fit on a scatter diagram?

Badger Key Stage 4 Maths Starters

Time series

Umbrella sales (recorded in thousands)

Year	2002				2003				2004				2005			
Quarter	1	2	3	4	1	2	3	4	1	2	3	4	1	2	3	4
Sales	43	19	8	17	41	17	5	15	44	19	10	18	46	21	12	21

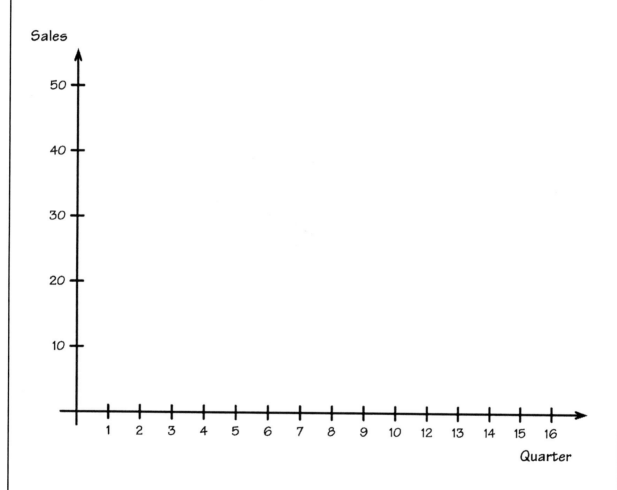

Year 11 Maths Starter 71 — Handling Data

Moving averages

Objective:

Calculate a moving average and make predictions.

Grade: C

What you will need:
OHT 71

Time:
5-10 minutes

Key words:

data, hypothesis, plot, time series, line graph, trend line

Activity:

Show OHT 71. Ask the students:

Q: What does this table show us? How is it conveying this information? For how many years do we have sales information? Why do you think the first quarter of the second year is given as the 5th quarter? Why have they not labelled this 1? Why might a company review sales patterns over a two year period instead of year-by-year? What trends can we identify in their sales figures for this two-year period? Can we say more than simply 'sales went up'? Can we calculate an average ~ or a series of averages ~ to help? What was the average sales of PCs for the first four quarters?

Give students 1-2 minutes to calculate the average. (34)

Q: Thirty-four what? (PCs) What average might we calculate next? Will simply calculating an average for sales during the 5th to 8th quarters tell the full story? Are there any other averages between the 1st and 8th quarters that might help? Why might it be useful to calculate average sales for the 2nd to 5th quarters? Which average could we calculate after that?

Give students 4-5 minutes to calculate the moving averages. (35.5, 35.75, 38.75, 39.75)

Links to plenary:

Q: Were they simple calculations? What do the moving averages tell us? What do I mean by 'moving' averages? Do they, on average, break the 40 PC mark? In which quarter do sales begin to increase? Does the increase hold steady?

Badger Key Stage 4 Maths Starters

© Badger Publishing Ltd

Moving averages

Quarter	1	2	3	4	5	6	7	8
PC sales per quarter	33	36	27	40	38	38	39	44

Year 11 Maths Starter 72 | **Handling Data**

Draw histograms

Objective:
Understand definition of and use of frequency density; use frequency density to construct histograms for grouped continuous data.

Grade: A

What you will need:
OHT 72

Time: 5-10 minutes

Key words:
data, continuous data, bar-chart, frequency, histogram, class interval, frequency density

Activity:

Show OHT 72. Refer to the table and bar-chart, ask the students:

Q: Is the bar-chart shown a fair and accurate representation of the data given in the table?

Give students 1-2 minutes to discuss this in pairs.

Q: Fair and accurate? Why not? What do you notice about the class intervals for the data given? What do I mean by 'class intervals'? Does it matter that they are uneven? Why does it look as if the first bar is representing far more people than the second bar? Can you use the word 'area' in your explanation? How could we correct this?

Again, give students 1-2 minutes to discuss this in pairs.

Q: If the class intervals are unequal, should we ensure that the area of bars is proportional to the frequency? How could we do this?

Links to plenary:

Q: What measure defines the width of the bars? (Width of class interval) Height? (Frequency) Can we divide the frequency by the width of class interval? Will that give us fairer heights for the bars? What should we label the vertical axis of our new histogram?

Badger Key Stage 4 Maths Starters

© Badger Publishing Ltd

Year 11: Copymaster for Starter 72 (OHT)
Draw histograms

Weight of Year 11 students

Weight	Frequency
$50 < w \le 70$kg	60
$70 < w \le 80$kg	72
$80 < w \le 85$kg	63

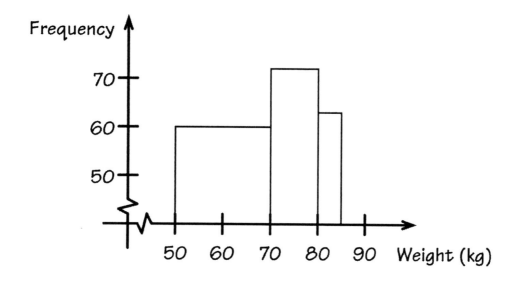

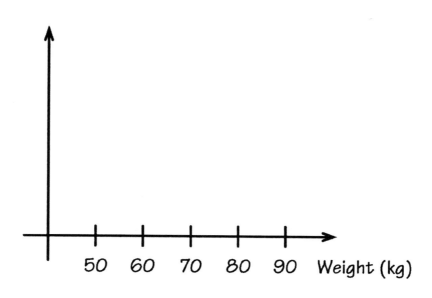

Badger Key Stage 4 Maths Starters

Year 11 Maths Starter 73 — Handling Data

Interpret histograms

Objective:
Use frequency density to construct histograms for grouped continuous data.

Grade: A

What you will need:
OHT 73

Time:
5-10 minutes

Key words:
data, continuous data, bar-chart, frequency, histogram, class interval, frequency density

Activity:

Show OHT 73. Ask the students:

Q: What is the OHT showing? What data does the histogram represent? How do we read this histogram? What information would I want to derive from it? How would we calculate the frequencies from a histogram where the vertical scale gives us the frequency density?

Give students 1-2 minutes to discuss this in pairs.

Q: How could we do it? What formula did we use to calculate frequency density for drawing a histogram? How could we change the subject of the formula to derive the frequencies?

Give students 3-4 minutes to calculate the frequencies for the given histogram.

Links to plenary:

Q: How did you do it? Were they relatively simple calculations? Which was the modal class? How could we derive an estimate for the mean from a histogram? What grade do you think this corresponds to? How do we remember the formula for deriving frequency density?

Badger Key Stage 4 Maths Starters

© Badger Publishing Ltd

Year 11: Copymaster for Starter 73 (OHT)
Interpret histograms

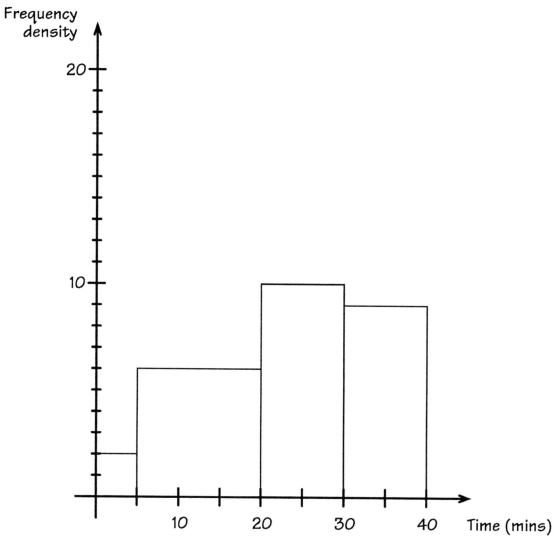

Time taken to complete homework

Year 11 Maths Starter 74 Handling Data

Relative frequencies

Objective:
Estimate probabilities and use relative frequencies to make predictions or test for bias.

Grade: C

What you will need:
OHT 74

Time: 5-10 minutes

Key words:
probability, event, outcome, numerator, denominator, frequency, relative frequency, theoretical probability, experimental probability

Activity:

Show OHT 74. Referring to the first table, ask the students:

Q: What do you notice about the data shown in the table? How has this data been derived? Has it been derived by using the theoretical probability for expected outcomes for throwing a dice? What do I mean by 'theoretical probability'? What other types of probability are there? How many times was the dice thrown for this table? Can we call that the number of trials? If the dice was a fair dice, roughly how many of each of the different outcomes would you expect to record? What can we say about this dice? Suppose we use an unfair dice ~ can we predict what the outcomes might be? What's the probability that we'll score a 5 on this dice? How could we use the experimental data to decide?

Give students 1-2 minutes to discuss this in pairs.

Q: How could we do it? True or false: 'Roughly $\frac{1}{4}$ of the throws gave us a score of 5.' Can we get a more accurate probability? Will it be appropriate to use a calculator? How could we use this skill to answer the exam question shown on the OHT?

Give students 1-2 minutes to attempt the question.

Links to plenary:

Q: How did you do it? What fractions were you calculating? Which numbers did you divide? How did you give the probabilities? How can we remember this skill? What grade do you think it corresponds to? Is it more likely to appear on the calculator paper?

Badger Key Stage 4 Maths Starters

© Badger Publishing Ltd

Year 11: Copymaster for Starter 74 (OHT)
Relative frequencies

Score	Frequency
one	22
two	15
three	23
four	18
five	28
six	14

The table shows the numbers of people that gave responses to the question:

'Should school term times change?'

Response	Yes	No	Don't know
Frequency	34	63	12

Calculate the probability that a person chosen at random will say 'yes'.

Answer: ....   *(2 marks)*

Badger Key Stage 4 Maths Starters

Year 11 Maths Starter 75 | **Handling Data**

Tree diagrams

Objective:
Complete tree diagrams as a means of showing outcomes for two successive events and related probabilities.

Grade: C/B

What you will need:
OHT 75

Time:
5-10 minutes

Key words:
probability, event, outcome, numerator, denominator, sample space, tree diagram

Activity:
Ask the students:

Q: If I throw a coin, what are the two possible outcomes? What do I mean by 'outcomes'? Suppose I throw a coin and then throw it again. What are the possible outcomes of two successive events like this? What do I mean by 'successive events'? If one possible outcome is that I throw a head followed by another head, what other outcomes are possible? How could we draw a diagram to record all the possible outcomes? Why do we need to know all the possible outcomes for an event? What will it help us to calculate?

Show OHT 75.

Q: Why might this be called a 'tree diagram'? How might we use this to record the outcomes for the first throw and then the second? Where could I record the four outcomes? Where could I record probabilities for each individual outcome? The four overall outcomes? If the probability of throwing a head is $\frac{1}{2}$, a tail is $\frac{1}{2}$, and these probabilities are repeated for the second branches of the diagram, how are they being combined to give us the overall probabilities for the two events? What do you notice?

Links to plenary:
Q: How might the probabilities P(H) = $\frac{1}{2}$ and P(H) = $\frac{1}{2}$ be combined to derive the probability of a head followed by another head, $\frac{1}{4}$? What can we do with the tree diagram that we couldn't do with the sample space diagram? What if the outcomes for a single event weren't equally likely?

Badger Key Stage 4 Maths Starters

© Badger Publishing Ltd

Year 11: Copymaster for Starter 75 (OHT)
Tree diagrams

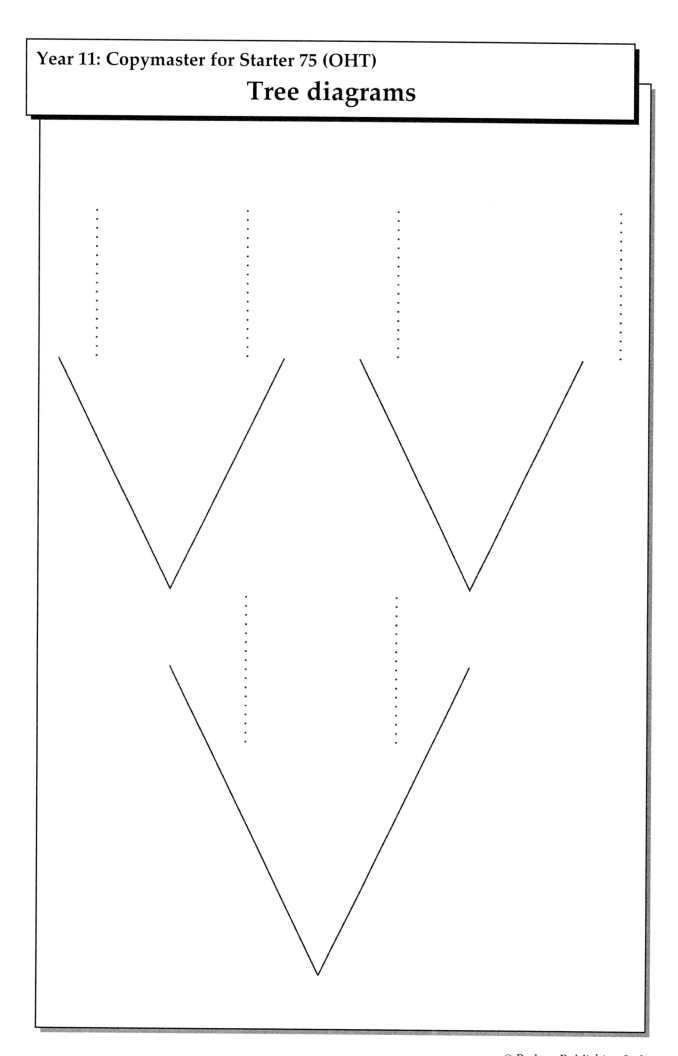

Year 11 Maths Starter 76   Handling data

The 'AND' rule

Objective:
Know when to use the P(A) + P(B) 'OR' rule, and the P(A) x (B) 'AND' rule.

Grade: B

What you will need:
OHT 76

Time:
5-10 minutes

Key words:
probability, event, outcome, numerator, denominator, sample space, tree diagram, independent, mutually exclusive

Activity:

Ask the students:

Q: Give me an example of an event that we quite often see used to devise probability problems. Why is throwing a coin or a dice used so often? What's important about the possible outcomes of those events - supposing they are fair? Imagine two events: I throw a dice and then I throw the dice again. Are these *independent* events? What do I mean by 'independent events'? Is the outcome of the second throw in any way dependent on the outcome of the first?

OK. I have a pack of cards. Can you give me two events that *aren't* independent? Why is the second pick conditional on the first? Imagine I throw the dice twice. I want a four on the first throw, then a five on the second. What's the probability of that outcome?

Give students 1-2 minutes to discuss this in pairs.

Q: How many possible outcomes are there for two throws of a dice? If we drew a sample space diagram, how many cells would it have? So is (4,5) one outcome out of 36? What's the probability of throwing a 5 on a dice? The probability of throwing a 4? How are these two combined to give us $\frac{1}{36}$? What's the probability of throwing a four *and* a five in that order?

Links to plenary:

Show OHT 76. Ask the students:

Q: How could we use the **AND** rule to solve this exam question? Are the two events independent? What's the probability that the train will be late on Tuesday? Wednesday? How do we combine those probabilities to find the probability that it will be late on Tuesday *and* Wednesday?

Badger Key Stage 4 Maths Starters

© Badger Publishing Ltd

Year 11: Copymaster for Starter 76 (OHT)

The 'AND' rule

The probability that, on any week day, the Hendon train is on time is 0.94.

Find the probability that the train is late on Tuesday and Wednesday.

Answer: . . . .   *(2 marks)*

Badger Key Stage 4 Maths Starters

Year 11 Maths Starter 77 Handling data

The 'OR' rule

Objective:

Know when to use the P(A) + P(B) 'OR' rule, and the P(A) x (B) 'AND' rule.

Grade: B

What you will need:
No additional resources.

Time:
5-10 minutes

Key words:
probability, event, outcome, numerator, denominator, sample space, tree diagram, independent, mutually exclusive

Activity:

Ask the students:

Q: Imagine two students are playing a game. They are each going to throw a dice. Julia needs to throw a five or a six to win. Is it possible to throw a five and a six at the same time? So these two outcomes are mutually exclusive. What do I mean by 'mutually exclusive'? Does she care whether it's a five or a six, as long as it's one of them? What's the probability that Julia will get the outcome that she wants? How did you decide?

So the probability of scoring a five *or* a six is $\frac{2}{6}$ or $\frac{1}{3}$. How have the probabilities for each of the two possible outcomes been combined to give us the probability that one *or* the other will happen? If I pick a card from an ordinary pack of cards, what's the probability that I'll pick a spade *or* a diamond? How did you decide?

Links to plenary:

Q: OK. I pick a card and keep it. Then I pick another. What's the probability that I pick a spade *and* a diamond? How is that problem different to the previous one? Does it matter whether I keep the card? How does it affect the probability of what happens next?

Badger Key Stage 4 Maths Starters

Year 11 Maths Starter 78	Handling data

Conditional probability

Objective:

Use the ideas of conditional probability to solve problems.

Grade: C

What you will need:
OHT 75

Time:
5-10 minutes

Key words:

probability, event, outcome, numerator, denominator, sample space, tree diagram, independent, mutually exclusive

Activity:

Show OHT 75 from the previous starter. Explain to the students:

Q: I want to use the tree diagram to look at two successive events. What will the tree diagram help us to find and calculate? How will it help us to establish all the possible outcomes? I want two events that are independent of each other. Give me some examples of such independent successive events. What grade do you think two successive independent events corresponds to? What about events that aren't independent? How does the idea that the second event is dependent on the first outcome make things more challenging? Can you give me an example of successive dependent events?

Suppose I have a bag of 12 coloured discs: 7 blue, 5 red. I choose a disc and record its colour, then put it back. Then I choose a second disc and record its colour. Are these two events dependent on each other? What one change could I make to my procedure to make them dependent on each other? How could we use the tree diagram to show the possible outcomes with their probabilities?

Give students 1-2 minutes to discuss this in pairs.

Links to plenary:

Q: How could we do it? What are the two possible outcomes for the first pick? Their probabilities? If I picked a blue disc on the first pick, is it still possible to pick either a blue or a red on the second? What's changed about the contents of the bag? What's the probability then that the second disc will be blue as well? Red? What's the probability that I'll pick a blue on the first pick *and* on the second? How do I combine the two probabilities on the tree diagram?

Badger Key Stage 4 Maths Starters

© Badger Publishing Ltd

For details of the full range of books and resources from

Badger Publishing

including

- Book Boxes for 11-16 and Special Needs
- Class sets of novels at great discounts
- KS3 Guided Reading Teacher Files and book packs
- Full Flight, Dark Flight, First Flight & Rex Jones for reluctant readers
- Brainwaves - non-fiction to get your brain buzzing
- Between the Lines - course exploring text types at KS3
- SAT Attack - Badger English and Maths Test Revision Guides
- Main Activity: Problem Solved! - KS3 Maths problem solving course
- Badger Literacy, Maths and Science Starters for KS3
- Badger Starters for the Foundation Subjects - History, Geography, Religious Education, Music, Design & Technology, Modern Foreign Languages - for KS3
- Badger Starters for the Interactive Whiteboard
- Badger Maths Starters for KS4
- Science Level-Assessed Tasks for KS3
- Badger ICT - lesson plans for KS3
- Badger Music - lesson plans for KS3
- Building Blocks History - complete unit for KS3
- Under the Skin - progressive plays for KS3
- Badger GSCE Religious Studies - illustrated textbooks
- Surviving Citizenship @ KS4
- Multiple Learning Activities - providing for different learning preferences
- Thinking Together in Geography - developing thinking skills

CD versions of many titles also now available.

See our full colour catalogue (available on request) or visit our website for more information:

www.badger-publishing.co.uk

Contact us at:

Badger Publishing Limited
15 Wedgwood Gate, Pin Green Industrial Estate,
Stevenage, Hertfordshire SG1 4SU
Telephone: 01438 356907
Fax: 01438 747015
enquiries@badger-publishing.co.uk

Or visit our showroom and bookshop at the above address.